REVEALING ANTIQUITY 19

G. W. BOWERSOCK, GENERAL EDITOR

SPARTACUS

ALDO SCHIAVONE

TRANSLATED BY **JEREMY CARDEN**

HARVARD UNIVERSITY PRESS

Cambridge, Massachusetts · London, England · 2013

Library of Congress Cataloging-in-Publication Data

Schiavone, Aldo.
    [Spartaco. English]
    Spartacus / Aldo Schiavone ; translated by Jeremy Carden.
      pages cm
    Includes bibliographical references and index.
    "Originally published as Spartaco . . . 2011 by Giulio Einudi
Editore SpA, Torino"—Title page verso.
    ISBN 978-0-674-05778-4 (alkaline paper)
    1. Spartacus, d. 71 B.C. 2. Slaves—Rome—Biography.
3. Gladiators—Rome—Biography. 4. Soldiers—Rome—
Biography. 5. Rome—History—Servile Wars, 135–71 B.C.
6. Slave insurrections—Rome. I. Title.
DG258.5.S3513   2013
937.05092—dc23
[B]   2012038240

CONTENTS

PREFACE TO THE AMERICAN EDITION

In the tradition of the West, Spartacus is a figure of the collective memory much more than of academic history. A character rather than a person, and a typically American character at that: a kind of indomitable hero of the frontier (albeit an ethical and mental frontier instead of a geographic one), a man who makes the difference and is prepared to die for a good cause. Stanley Kubrick was quite aware of this when he directed his celebrated film. The fortunes of such a construction have been significantly shaped, both by the romantic vision of history and by the recurrent interpretation that considers the potent and compelling paradigm of the class struggle as a universal key for understanding human events—two weighty legacies of nineteenth-century Europe, and interconnected much more than we are accustomed to think. Yet a substantial part of that image bathed in light had already formed outside of modernity; we owe it precisely to Spartacus's bitterest enemies, the Romans. In the following pages we will try to see how this came about.

The American edition would not have been possible without the help of many friends—above all, and once again, that of Glen Bowersock: my debt to him is unequalled, and to acknowledge it is for me a source of renewed joy. Then of all the people at Harvard University Press, especially Sharmila Sen, for the attention, professionalism, and warmth with which she has helped me over the years; and with them my translator, Jeremy Carden—by now my voice in English. And finally, Fara Nasti, who assisted me with the maps and in the final reading of the proofs. To them all, my most sincere thanks.

BEFORE BEGINNING . . .

This book is not about the legend of Spartacus. It is a biographical tale, sticking closely to the historical facts. At the same time, an effort has been made to bring out the wider context around the protagonist, which alone can restore a comprehensible meaning to his actions. It was a background dominated by a phenomenon as atrocious as it was complex: imperial Roman slavery, in an age—the seventh decade of the first century B.C.— and in places—the countryside and cities of central-southern Italy, by then completely Romanized—which saw the maximum diffusion of this terrible and invasive practice.

As with the other great figures who fought against the Roman empire—Hannibal, Jugurtha, Mithridates, Vercingetorix—everything we know about Spartacus comes to us from what was remembered of him by his mortal foes. The images preserved by ancient tradition are a reflection of the ones stamped in the minds of the victors. The stories surrounding his name are all Roman, or at least gathered by the Romans. And when speaking of their slaves, the ancients, who in many ways seem very close to us, suddenly reveal the abyss that separates them from our world.

The narratives relating to Spartacus were elaborated in particular in the years between Cicero and Augustus, in circles contiguous to the ruling groups. But of everything written on the subject by the two most important historians to treat the theme, and the nearest in time to the events, Sallust and Livy, there remain just a few fragments of the former and practically nothing of the latter. On the other hand, we are fairly well informed about virtually every aspect of the Roman history of that time: politics, economy, culture, sensibility, everyday life—almost no other period in antiquity is better known to us. In our reconstruction we have therefore been able to piece together a historic landscape—tensions, forces, possibilities, fractures—of unsuspected richness, and to introduce into the story a thread of clues and conjectures capable of transforming much of what was believed to be definitively lost information into merely hidden information that can still be brought to light. The result, hopefully, is a compact account readily accessible to readers—the goal of any genuine historical work.

Spartacus was not the commander of a people up in arms against Rome, such as the Carthaginians, Gauls, Numidians, or the populations of Illyria and Pontus.

These conflicts, however bitter, were a regular feature of the Roman conquerors' military routine. In the rise and consolidation of a world power, war and the physical annihilation of the enemy were considered inevitable, something to which the Romans had become accustomed: it was part of their everyday life. But Spartacus's defiance was a radically different matter, almost unspeakable for the dominant culture, the symbol of extreme subversion, of a dramatic break in the "natural" order of things, which translated bloodily and frighteningly into its inconceivable opposite. He was a slave in revolt, at the head of an army consisting largely of men in the same condition, who had succeeded in threatening the very heart of the imperial system.

Slavery was an all-encompassing and totally pervasive institution in Rome. It was not only essential from an economic point of view, but touched on every strand of the civil, moral, and emotional experience of society: from family life to the imagination, sexuality to leisure—just as would happen, almost two thousand years later, in the southern states of America before the Civil War, described, with an observant and troubled gaze, by Alexis de Tocqueville in the diaries of his American travels. The numbers alone give us an idea of things: in the first century B.C., in Italy, more or less in the same years as Spartacus, about a third of the whole population was made up of slaves—millions of slaves. But unlike capitalist and industrial America, which could turn to other very different models and alternatives, in the culture of Roman Italy and of the

Mediterranean, a society without slave labor was literally unthinkable. And the rebels themselves, as we shall see, were blinkered by the same insurmountable mental block. This too was an intrinsic part of the empire, just as it was of what has come to be known as "classical" antiquity.

Mario Citroni and Andrea Giardina read a draft version of this book. Their observations, invaluable as ever, avoided some errors and contributed—within the limits of the possible—to improving it.

Francesca Tamburi helped in the revision of the manuscript. My heartfelt thanks to them all.

All the dates, unless otherwise specified, are B.C.

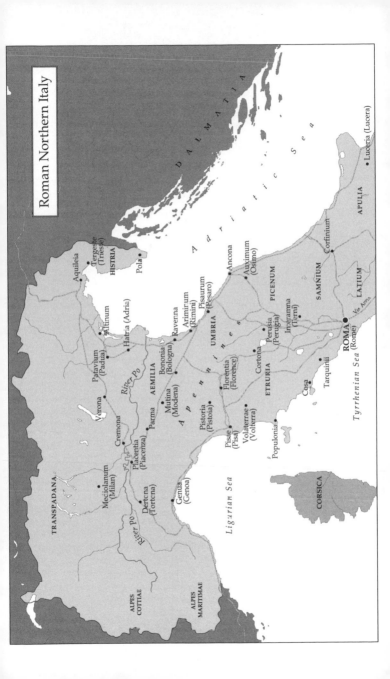

Roman Northern Italy

DALMATIA

Adriatic Sea

TRANSPADANA

ALPES COTTIAE

ALPES MARITIMAE

Aquileia
Tergeste (Trieste)
HISTRIA
Pola
Altinum
Hatria (Adria)
Patavium (Padua)
Verona
Cremona
Meciolanum (Milan)
Placentia (Piacenza)
Dertena (Tortona)
Genua (Genoa)
River Po
AEMILIA
Parma
Mutina (Modena)
Bononia (Bologna)
Ravenna
Arimirum (Rimini)
Pisaurum (Pesaro)
UMBRIA
A p e n n i n e s
Florentia (Florence)
Pistoria (Pistoia)
Pisae (Pisa)
Volaterrae (Volterra)
Populonia
Cortona
Perusia (Perugia)
ETRURIA
Cosa
Tarquinii
Interamna (Terni)
Ancona
Auximum (Osimo)
PICENUM
SAMNIUM
Corfinium
LATIUM
ROMA (Rome)
Via Appia
APULIA
Luceria (Lucera)

Tyrrhenian Sea

Ligurian Sea

CORSICA

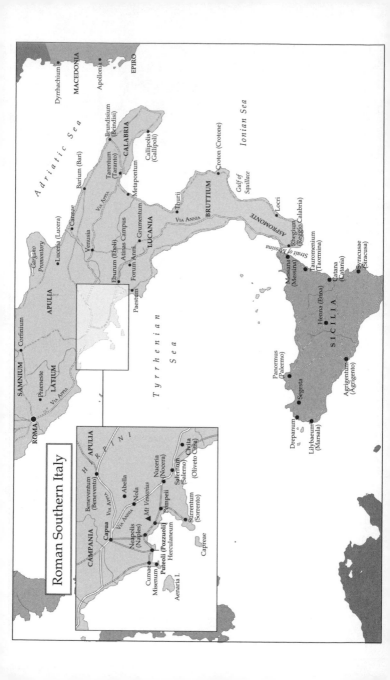

Roman Southern Italy

EPIRO
MACEDONIA
Dyrrhachium
Apollonia

Adriatic Sea

Lucera (Lucera)
Cannae
Barium (Bari)
Brundisium (Brindisi)
CALABRIA
Gargano Promontory
Tarentum (Taranto)
Metapontum
Callipolis (Gallipoli)
Venusia
Via Appia
Croton (Crotone)

Ionian Sea

Corfinium
SAMNIUM
APULIA
Eburum (Eboli)
Atinas Campus
LUCANIA
Via Annia
Thurii
BRUTTIUM
Gulf of Squillace
LATIUM
Praeneste
Forum Ann.
Paestum
Locri
ASPROMONTE
Via Appia
ROMA

Tyrrhenian Sea

Strait of Messina
Messana (Messina)
Rhegium (Reggio Calabria)
Tauromenium (Taormina)
Catana (Catania)
Syracusae (Siracusa)
Henna (Enna)
SICILIA
Panormus (Palermo)
Segesta
Agrigentum (Agrigento)
Drepanum
Lilybaeum (Marsala)

Inset: Roman Southern Italy (detail)

APULIA
H I R P I N I
Beneventum (Benevento)
Via Appia
Abella
Nuceria (Nocera)
Civita (Civita Gitta)
CAMPANIA
Capua
Via Annia
Nola
Salernum (Salerno)
Neapolis (Naples)
Mt Vesuvius
Pompeii
Surrentum (Sorrento)
Cumae
Misenum
Puteoli (Pozzuoli)
Herculaneum
Capreae
Aenaria I.

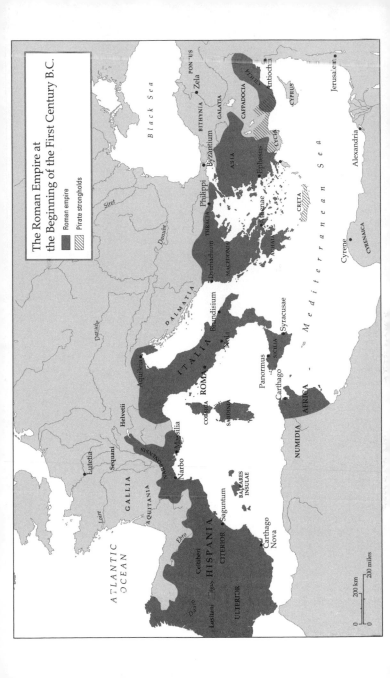

The Roman Empire at
the Beginning of the First Century B.C.

████ Roman empire
▨▨▨ Pirate strongholds

ATLANTIC OCEAN

Black Sea

Mediterranean Sea

GALLIA
AQUITANIA
Lutetia
Sequani
Helvetii
Massilia
Narbo
NARBONENSIS

HISPANIA
Celtiberi
Lusitani
CITERIOR
ULTERIOR
Saguntum
Carthago Nova
BALEARES INSULAE

ITALIA
ROMA
Brundisium
Nola
Aquileia
DALMATIA
CORSICA
SARDINIA
SICILIA
Panormus
Syracusae

AFRICA
NUMIDIA
Carthago
CYRENAICA
Cyrene

MACEDONIA
Dyrrachium
Philippi
THRACE
Byzantium
BITHYNIA
PONTUS
Zela
GALATIA
CAPPADOCIA
ASIA
Ephesus
LYCIA
CILICIA
Antioch
CYPRUS
CRETA
Athenae

Alexandria
Jerusalem

Duero
Tagus
Ebro
Loire
Siret
Danube
Drave

0   200 km
0   200 miles

SPARTACUS

ONE

THE FUGITIVE

· 1 ·

E<small>VERYTHING</small> was going well, just as they had hoped. They had slithered quickly down the high, steep rock face and gathered in silence at the bottom, not far from the Roman camp. It must have been close to sunrise— such a dangerous descent could not conceivably have been attempted in pitch darkness. It is likely instead that they had chosen the first glimmer of dawn, with some light already, but the Romans still deep in slumber. It was not cold, though the nights are always cool on Mount Vesuvius.

It was here, in fact, that they had taken refuge (as we are told by Appian and Florus; Plutarch, who relates the episode better, does not specify where). And it was here that they had been hunted down by troops sent from Rome to follow their trail. But now they were turning the mountain that had sheltered them into a mortal trap for the pursuers.

The topography of the area is different today, partly due to two millennia of lava accumulation, and this does not help us to identify the spot exactly: one plausible hypothesis is that the fugitives hid out in the hills between Mounts Somma and Vesuvius. The volcano, more than a thousand meters high, had at any rate been inactive for centuries—a deceptive, albeit protracted calm: less than 150 years later a massive eruption would bury Herculaneum and Pompeii.

The plan had taken shape almost by chance: a small masterpiece of quick-witted exploitation of local resources, available skills, and the circumstances of the moment, destined to be remembered in the military chronicles of the ancients, and still recalled by Frontinus in a passage from his *Stratagems*.

The crest of the mount where they had retreated, practically besieged, abounded in wild vines: the slopes of Vesuvius were clad with vineyards, which produced a celebrated wine described by Cicero as one of the wonders of "arrogant" Campania. And so the sinewy branches had been fashioned into long, flexible ladders, enabling them, from the summit, to get down over the rocks into the bottom of the gorge, instead of taking the only existing path, thereby eluding the Roman surveillance. Some of the fugitives had worked in the local countryside, and knew how to weave wicker baskets. Perhaps everything was done in just one night, so the besiegers did not get wind of what was going on.

Now was the moment to lower the weapons, followed by the last remaining people at the top. A concealed track across the rugged slopes, known to someone in the group (perhaps from among those who had woven the ladders), took them straight to the rear of the Roman force, which was "several cohorts" strong, as we are again informed by Frontinus, and commanded by the praetor (or possibly propraetor) Caius Claudius Glaber—not exactly a military talent.

The Romans had pitched camp facing what they considered to be the only practicable—and in any case narrow and rough—way to the top, so as not to leave the fugitives any escape route. But they had seriously underestimated the imagination and aggressiveness of their quarry; and it is likely they had not even fortified their position, as was standard practice, betrayed by the inexperience of the commander and overconfidence in their undoubted superiority of numbers: several thousand against no more than a few hundred fugitives (there is considerable disagreement about this second figure, but the dynamics of the events and the configuration of the terrain, as described by the ancient authors, make it hard to believe there were any more).

Attacked suddenly from the rear—with many perhaps still asleep—by men trained in ferocious hand-to-hand fighting, the Romans did not have a chance. The tactical surprise was complete. There was not even a real battle. The camp was overrun, and the soldiers killed or put to flight. In the space of a few hours, the siege had been broken.

When it was all over, the sun must have been rising over the horizon, bathing in light and warmth a landscape in which harsh, dark lava gave way to pale, attractive softness: woods and vineyards all around, Herculaneum below, Pompeii a little to the south, and, just beyond, the Gulf of Naples between Capri and Cape Misenum.

The day had yielded a victor, the man who had inspired and led the escape, and probably devised the astute plan. Unhoped-for possibilities now opened up before him. He was still free, a man of arms in his physical and mental prime—he was probably no more than thirty years of age. It would in fact be hard to imagine him being any older—life expectancy, for those in his position, did not stretch much beyond that. His name, Latinized, was Spartacus; for the Romans, his masters, it was now the name of a runaway slave, a wretch for whom nothing remained but death.

It was the beginning of the summer of 73 (all dates in this book, unless otherwise specified, are B.C.)—680 years since the foundation of Rome.

· 2 ·

Everything had started a few weeks earlier, in a prison-training camp for gladiators—a *ludus,* a gym, as it was then called—on the outskirts of Capua.

The city, about twenty kilometers north of Naples, was one of the most important in southern Italy, and among the most densely populated in the Italic Peninsula. Described by Cicero several decades later as a place of "pride and dissoluteness," but also "one of the most beautiful in Italy," its urban layout, on a magnificent plain, pleased its "haughty" inhabitants, who greatly preferred it to Rome itself, "all hills, valleys, and narrow alleys." The famous Appian Way linked it directly to the capital, and an excellent network of local roads ensured regular contact with other centers in Campania, especially Puteoli (Pozzuoli) and its port, along an axis stretching as far as Herculaneum and Pompeii on the opposite side of the Gulf of Naples. And even if its integration into the institutional and civil fabric of Roman Italy had been marked by a serious political misadventure, when, immediately after the disaster of Cannae in 216, Capua had abandoned its alliance with Rome and sided with Hannibal, the city's development, which dated back to a very early Etruscan presence, had never really been interrupted. The Romans did not forget the betrayal, but had cautiously gotten over it, though not before meting out severe punishment. Now, in the heart of the first century, Capua seemed to have reached its peak: wheat, wine, fabrics, meat, metals, and perfumes were regularly exported to the rest of Campania and to Rome, if, that is, they were not shipped, via Puteoli, for trade across the Mediterranean.

But we must be careful not to exaggerate when imagining the riches evoked by the ancients. Their words can lead us astray, because they refer to magnitudes that are not ours. Their experience of abundance, and especially its diffusion, was incommensurably different from that of the modern West. The classical world never had what we might narrowly define as industrial cities—and therefore not their well-being either—just agricultural and trading centers that sold excess farm produce (what was not needed for domestic consumption) and the goods turned out by small factories or craft workshops. Although profits were sometimes quite considerable, providing a fair degree of comfort for some strands of society, with scattered peaks of genuine opulence, the overriding problem for most inhabitants in any ancient city was to find, before sundown, sufficient food to stave off hunger and to survive.

Like all the most important places in Roman Italy, perhaps even more so, Capua was also a city of slaves. They arrived both from the capital, and, undoubtedly (again through Puteoli), from Delos, the most important slave market in the Mediterranean, where, it was said, up to ten thousand prisoners might be sold in a day. It is difficult to give an accurate figure for Capua itself and the area immediately around it—there was no census of slaves, because they were not part of the community, they were excluded from civil society. But in the years of our story it must have run into many thousands: probably not less than a third of the whole population (though this is unlikely to have been as much as fifty thousand).

Sometimes, slaves attempted to escape, or to rebel, and were harshly punished for it. Puteoli had a pivotal role in such repression, which involved the use of real professionals (one specialist, the *fugitivarius,* was generally charged with the task of capturing the reprobate). A municipal regulation, reproduced on an epigraph, and attributable to a period not far off the one we are dealing with, describes in detail the obligations of the contractor chosen by the culprit's owner to prepare the punishment, which was to take place before the whole community: building of the gallows, performance of the crucifixion, payment of the executioners—four sesterces, a little more than the pay of a workshop laborer. Not long afterward, a great jurist, and friend of Caesar, took pains to clarify who exactly should be considered a "fugitive" (slave), and was therefore liable to suffer the consequences: it was someone, he wrote, who stayed away from his owner's house in a deliberate effort to keep away from him.

The slaves did not just work on farm estates or in the related manufactories (though this was the lot of the great majority), or in the workshops and households of the city, at the service—with a disparate range of duties—of their owners. A small number were reserved for another kind of activity: for combat in the arena—in those spectacles (*circenses*, but the expression referred principally to horse races) that the Roman people, according to a celebrated line of verse by Juvenal (composed, in truth, over a century later), were unable, together with bread, to do without: "panem et circenses."

Spartacus had been one of them.

· 3 ·

In Capua, several training camps for gladiators probably existed at the time. Caesar himself would later open one. A salubrious climate and proximity to Rome were factors encouraging their establishment; and from what Livy says, there seems to have been an ancient tradition of these "games" in the city, dating back as far as the fourth century—when Capua had just entered the sphere of Roman control—perhaps initiated to celebrate a victory against the hated Samnites.

The camp Spartacus was in would not have differed much from the two buildings uncovered at Pompeii: a cross between a prison and a fortress. It was kept by a certain Gnaeus Lentulus Batiatus (though we are not entirely sure of the name): and the business might well have been a lucrative one (the person running it was called a *lanista,* a word which, in Latin, recalled the one for "butcher"; while *gladiator* designated someone who used a short sword, the *gladius,* in combat, and is the term already employed frequently in the second century to generically indicate anyone who fought in the arena). If the men trained for this purpose became famous and sought-after—the games were still privately organized in that period—the earnings for their owners would have been substantial.

In Rome, these spectacles were very popular. Virtually the sole source of socialization and entertainment for the great urban masses, they punctuated the rhythm of city life, and fueled an inexhaustible flow of collective fantasies. They had been introduced for the first time in 264 (we are indebted to Valerius Maximus for the precision of the date), at the beginning of the First Punic War, in the course of a funeral ceremony laid on in the Forum Boarium by a prominent aristocratic family to celebrate the memory of the late head of the household. The novelty recalled practices current in other areas of Italy (Capua has already been mentioned), again possibly associated with funeral rites. But in Rome, the success that immediately transformed it into a real vogue was also the sign of a change in the customs of the city, where the leading noble families did not disdain the opportunities such occasions provided to publicly flaunt their more or less recently acquired wealth in order to build political consensus. For the funeral of Publius Licinius Crassus in 183, for instance, no less than sixty pairs of gladiators faced up to each other in a dazzling series of fights—no one could remember having seen anything like it.

In the organization of the spectacles, however, the new social ostentation was also accompanied by the resurfacing of older emotions, linked, originally, to a kind of collective exorcism of death—that of the deceased person who was being celebrated—through the staging of other (possible) deaths—those of the combatants in the games. Death against death: a long-standing connection in the Mediterranean aristocracies—there are already traces of it in the *Iliad*. And it is likely that in Rome, at least at the beginning of this tradition, the blood shed by the gladiators really did stir memories, in the deepest layers of popular emotion, of the performance of a genuine sacrificial ritual, in which the victim was now embodied by the defeated fighter. New habits and old remembrances. In fact, it was precisely the purifying power of a death, crystallized and repeated in the transfiguration of an extremely ancient ceremony, that could be found in the very earliest nucleus of Roman religiosity: when the supreme head of the city, the king, sacrificed a ram (described as the leader of the flock) on the altar, establishing an identification revelatory of an evident symbolic shift—from the king to the ram, from the community to the flock—as Varro had already perceptively noted.

But this undercurrent had then gradually disappeared, covered over by other emotions and other mental associations. Rome had managed to amply compensate for its original syndrome of insecurity, that of an unstable and besieged community terrorized by its own divinities (as Polybius was to write), surrounded by perils and foes—Sabines, Latins, Etruscans, Samnites, Gauls, Carthaginians—and to turn it around into a symmetrically opposite collective impulse toward domination and conquest, which would accompany and orient its imperial ascent. Success after success, the need to feel secure had been transformed into the need for expansion, into an irresistible drive to acquire more and more space. An enterprising and compact nobility had succeeded in unifying around this mass reflex the whole of republican society.

And so began that terrible love of war and of glory in battle as an extreme form of competitive rivalry among the aristocracy, that irresistible inclination toward the "martial state of soul," with the consequent and almost automatic willingness of every citizen to put their life at stake for the sake of the republic—in a word, the consolidation of military practice as the foundation of all civil experience—that would mark the history of Rome forever and would be quite familiar to Sallust and Tacitus.

It was in this intrinsically violent context, where the routine of war and the accumulation of related fantasies had become one of the main emotional driving forces in society, that gladiatorial shows had, by the middle of the second century, found a place in the heart of popular sensibility, transformed into a custom that had already sparked the irony of the peaceable Terence. Increasingly detached from funerary rites and memories of sacrifice, they were now a stable component in the experience of the festivity, of the spectacle, of city munificence—of the heady sharing in the pleasure of blood and its contaminating heat.

In this way gladiators even entered the dreams of the masses. Artemidorus, in his extraordinary oneiric catalogue—a window on the classic unconscious, despite the literary reelaboration of the materials—composed around the middle of the second century A.D., when the games had spread all over the empire, elegantly records the trace of this invasive nocturnal presence: "Fighting [in a dream] as a gladiator signifies that a man will be involved in a lawsuit, or will fight in some other dispute or battle. In fact, a trial is also called a 'fight,' even though it is not fought with weapons, which signify the documents and legal claims of those fighting. The weapons of the man pursued always signify the defendant, the weapons of the pursuer signify the plaintiff." Arms and law, then; the first as the metaphor and oneiric guise of the second: an ingenuous yet brilliant interpretative association that linked, in the superimposition of contiguous images, the two most authentic Roman vocations.

· 4 ·

Until the beginning of the first century, the fighters were all prisoners of war: enemies or foreigners reduced to slavery. Gladiatorial combat had a marked ethnic trait, linked to the names of defeated or "barbarian" populations—the "Samnite," the "Thracian," the "Gaul" (Gallic gladiators were definitely present in Rome from 186). Then something changed, a significant mutation that was witnessed by Cicero:

> What wounds will the gladiators bear, who are either barbarians, or the very dregs of mankind! How do they, who are trained to it, prefer being wounded to basely avoiding it! How often do they prove that they consider nothing but giving satisfaction to their masters or to the people! For when covered with wounds, they send to their masters to learn their pleasure: if it be their will, they are ready to lie down and die. What gladiators, of even moderate reputation, ever gave a sigh? Who ever turned pale? Who ever disgraced himself either in the actual combat, or even when about to die? Who that had been defeated ever drew in his neck to avoid the stroke of death? So great is the force of practice, deliberation, and custom! Shall this, then, be done by "A Samnite

rascal, worthy of his trade" [here Cicero cites a line from Lucilius], and shall a man born to glory have so soft a part in his soul as not to be able to fortify it by reason and reflection? The sight of the gladiators' combats is by some looked on as cruel and inhuman, and I do not know, as it is at present managed, but it may be so; but when only the guilty fought . . . there was no better training to harden us against pain and death.

What disturbed Cicero is that when he was writing, between 45 and 44, there were no longer just "barbarian" slaves fighting in the arena, as had once been the case, but Roman citizens as well. Having lost everything, they sold themselves—their honor and freedom—and, with a kind of legally recognized oath, surrendered themselves up of their own free will into the hands of a *lanista,* an impresario. For Cicero this radically altered the civil quality of the representation, and its ethical import. If Roman citizens were fighting each other—however degrading that might be—it was possible to accept, if not necessarily to share, feelings of pity and reprobation for the ferocity of the combat. But the solidarity only extended to citizens: it could not go beyond that, it could not include slaves. And yet it was precisely in that "beyond," in that no-man's-land where there was no room for any social tie, or for any compassion, that the moral significance of the spectacle was paradoxically determined. It consisted in the display of a kind of inflexible pedagogy, demonstrating cruelly but clearly that it was not so very difficult to face pain and death with fortitude. If slaves, admittedly well trained, did so, how could a Roman "born to glory" shrink from it when his time came?

The intense competitive rivalry among the aristocracy, as we have just said, conditioned the whole of society, and was fed by a propensity for violence and a scorn for human life rendered almost everyday by ceaseless campaigning and endless conquest ("wars that breed war," wrote Sallust in those years). It was just such a mind-set that lent legitimacy to gladiatorial combat and at the same time explained its success.

We can suppose that the change, with an increasing number of Roman citizens among the combatants, began precisely toward the middle of the first century, and that Cicero was a firsthand—and shocked—observer of its early appearance. Later it would be accepted without reservation: in the age of the Principate—when gladiatorial shows were at their most popular, having spread to all the major cities in the empire—the sight of free men fighting in the arena would not have represented a problem for anyone.

But at the beginning of the first century the gladiators were still almost entirely foreign slaves, and in the camps of Capua there were above all Gauls and Thracians. The presence of the latter in the arena was so frequent that, in the language of the games, the word indicating their origin ("Thracian") slowly lost its ethnic connotations and came to generically denote a type of combatant and the role he played in the dynamics of the spectacle (a bit like talking about a linebacker or a wide receiver today), irrespective of the gladiator's provenance. And it was like this—as a role and as a mask—that they continued to live on in the dreams recorded by Artemidorus. "I have often observed," continues the author on the same page cited earlier, "that this dream [of gladiators] indicates that a man will marry a woman whose character corresponds to the type of weapons that he dreams he is using or to the type of opponent against whom he is fighting. . . . For example, if a man fights with a Thracian, he will marry a wife who is rich, crafty, and fond of being first. She will be rich because the Thracian's body is entirely covered by his armor; crafty, because his sword is not straight; and fond of being first, because this fighter employs the advancing technique." This time the interpretative overlay—the presumed symbolic disclosure— is no longer between arms and law, but between combat and marriage, wife and enemy; equally ingenuous but no less effective in its hopeless machismo.

Spartacus was from Thrace. In the spectacles he must have been a "Thracian," possibly a *murmillo*—at any rate, a heavyweight.

· 5 ·

How he ended up in the hands of the Romans is unknown. Annaeus Florus, a historian writing in the years between Trajan and Hadrian who drew inspiration from Livy but sometimes turned to Sallust and Caesar as well, summed up concisely but evocatively what information he had: "[Spartacus] who, from being a Thracian tributary, had become a [Roman] soldier, and from a soldier a deserter, then a bandit, and finally, thanks to his strength, a gladiator" (an even more succinct summary can be found in Appian). It is a skeletal outline of a tempestuous life on the margins of the empire, briefly sketched and oozing with disdain (though Florus's appraisal does not end here, as we will see, a sign that he used different sources). Standing out is a damning word—*latro,* bandit, brigand, highwayman—already used for Spartacus by Cicero in the *Philippics.* Immediately afterward, as if that were not sufficient, Florus adds that he had led a life of "dishonor" *(dedecus).* Yet different, less prejudiced versions of the crucial episode of Spartacus's youth—his enslavement—must have started circulating almost immediately. Varro, for example, did not hesitate to talk of Spartacus as "innocent . . . thrown in among the gladiators." He was drawing on an evaluation almost certainly found in Sallust, and perhaps in Posidonius, a Greek philosopher and erudite close to the Roman aristocracy, who in those years had traveled the length and breadth of the Mediterranean, and had been profoundly disturbed by the plight of the toiling slave masses he had had occasion to see, a recent (and, for him, deplorable) product of the imperial conquests. A trace of Varro's judgment can be found at the beginning of Plutarch's account as well, probably also indebted to Sallust, when Spartacus and his companions are described as men who, "through no misconduct of theirs" and due entirely to the "injustice" of their owner, found themselves forced to fight in the arena.

But what was the chain of events referred to in Florus's bare sequence? Some elements of it can still be pieced together.

Like other young Thracians of his kind, Spartacus soon had dealings with the Romans, belonging as he did to a community that was already a tributary of the empire (I believe Florus's reference to his status as a *stipendiarius* must be understood in its civil rather than military sense, as "tributary" instead of "mercenary," as it is sometimes translated; otherwise, an unexplainable muddle would arise when he is then referred to as a "soldier," which, as he was not a Roman citizen, could mean nothing other than "mercenary." Moreover, Sulla, in those years, had contributed to reorganizing the fiscal arrangements in the Eastern provinces, and had probably increased the number of "tributaries" of Rome). When Spartacus came into contact with the Romans, he would have been little more than twenty years old—any other hypothesis would skew the whole chronology of his life. He must, then, have been born around 100, perhaps a little earlier.

In the eyes of the Greeks and Romans, Thrace appeared to be a vast, populous, and largely unknown country. Corresponding more or less to modern-day Bulgaria and the European part of Turkey, it lay northeast of what were the borders of the empire at the beginning of the first century: a land of rough shepherds and fierce warriors (especially on horseback), who lived for the most part in village communities and still had a tribal organization, though they were familiar with farming and metalworking. Herodotus had said of them that if they had joined forces under a single king, they would have been invincible—a view shared by Thucydides. Philip II, the father of Alexander the Great, conquered the whole region in the middle of the fourth century, and it remained within the Macedonian sphere of influence even after the collapse of Alexander's empire; this encouraged a few early seeds of urban development and made the Greek presence, limited until then to the coastal zones, more substantial.

Following the Roman victory at Pydna in 168, the area of the country to the west of the River Hebrus was incorporated into the newly established province of Macedonia, and a new road, the Via Egnatia, was soon built to link it to Dyrrhachium and Apollonia. The border with the Thracian territories outside the empire was never completely stabilized, however, what with continual raids by neighboring tribes and the ensuing punitive missions by the Romans, not always crowned by success. In one of these, in 114, the consul Gaius Porcius Cato was roundly defeated, and it was not until after 107 that the Romans managed to gain tighter though still not definitive control over the whole of southern Thrace, beyond the Macedonian border.

According to Plutarch, who once again drew on Sallust, Spartacus was "a Thracian of Maidi stock" (a people already known to Thucydides, settled in the southwest of the country right next to the imperial frontier, in an area already partly incorporated into Roman Macedonia, and often involved in bitter clashes with the imperial troops. However, the reading of the text is uncertain, and some experts have proposed "of nomadic stock," though this is a less probable hypothesis). He was "possessed not only of great courage and strength" (here the affirmation corresponds literally to a fragment in Sallust's *Histories*, where it is said that "he was endowed with an outstanding measure of strength and courage"), but also, continues Plutarch, again transcribing from Sallust, "in intelligence and gentleness superior to his condition, and more Hellenized than one would expect from his origin."

How should these words be interpreted? Certainly in the sense that, before encountering the Romans, the young Spartacus had had some contact with the Greeks, quickly learning to express himself well in their language: undoubtedly to read and probably to write it. Later on this would help him to learn Latin, in which he definitely became fluent. Might we even venture to think that he also became acquainted with books in his youth? This is hard to sustain, as such familiarity was very rare outside the big cities, and there is no evidence to suggest Spartacus ever visited any.

But Spartacus had also learnt what Plutarch described as "gentleness" *(praotēs)*. It is a surprising remark in the context of his life, and all the more reliable precisely for that reason. And it lifts the rapid Sallustian-Plutarchian sketch out of the ocean of stock stereotypes—of pure *remplissage*—in which ancient biography writing often flounders. For an instant, a whole inner world opens up before us. The fineness of mind to which Plutarch alludes undoubtedly formed part of the ideal type of Greek man, but it jars with the life of arms that Spartacus would soon take up—with the portrait of a ruthless and semibarbarous warrior. Instead, in a wholly unexpected manner, a more faceted personality takes shape, happily positioned between two cultures, if not between two anthropologies—Thracian strength and Greek gentleness: a difficult synthesis of unsuspected richness.

Rather more ambiguous is the reference to Spartacus's "condition" *(tychē)*. Was Plutarch speaking about his original social status in Thrace, or his acquired Roman one as a gladiator slave? Once again, it is hard to decide, though I would tend to opt for the second hypothesis: when he alludes to Spartacus's origins, Plutarch uses twice, in the same group of sentences, a different word: *ghenos* (stock). What those origins were is unclear: Mommsen went so far as to suggest a royal provenance—and he is not alone—but there is no evidence to confirm this.

Whatever his roots, this out-of-the-ordinary young man, who combined a number of contrasting talents, soon became a soldier in the Roman army *(miles,* says Florus). He may have been recruited in the years in which Sulla was in Greece and Macedonia—between 87 and 83, probably toward the middle or end of that period (Sulla was in Macedonia in 85)—during the first war against Mithridates, king of Pontus. The Romans, engaged in a difficult campaign of reconquest and containment—almost the whole of Greece had fallen into enemy hands—urgently needed to increase their combat strength, and the use of Thracian auxiliaries was certainly part of their strategy. The Thracians were highly skilled in fighting on horseback—Spartacus was no exception—and the Romans were accustomed to recruiting the majority of their cavalry from among foreign populations. Indeed, a Thracian cavalry unit ("ala Thracia") is known to have operated in Britain in the second half of the first century A.D.

What legion Spartacus belonged to is unknown. Epigraphic evidence attests to the existence, in the second half of the first century, of a Sixth Legion "Macedonica," but we are not in a position to say whether the name should be associated with the presence (and possibly the formation) of this unit in the places and period about which we are talking.

We will never know what led Spartacus to enroll, especially at a time when the whole of the East was seething with persistent anti-Roman feeling, culminating in the implacable hostility of Mithridates and the insurrection of Athens and Greece. Perhaps a youthful and irrepressible passion for arms, admiration for the warlike virtues of the people now perceived to be the masters of the world, or dreams of an adventurous life in the ranks of conquerors—or all those things together.

At any rate, they were decisive years for the young Spartacus, during which he completed his military apprenticeship and his character was shaped for good; years in which physical strength, ardor, intelligence, and fineness of spirit became firmly welded together, and he fully developed the potential to become a commander. The earlier Hellenistic influences would soon be overlaid by the effects of an intense Romanization. There is no indication as to what rank he held in Sulla's auxiliary forces. But in those times a Thracian cavalryman was considered an exceptional fighter of rare power, and undoubtedly his position would have enabled him to gain a thorough knowledge of the Roman military machine, to gauge its organization and effectiveness on the battlefield, to absorb its operative protocols firsthand, and to hone an aptitude for leadership that was soon to be displayed so brilliantly. Roman military technology, and the tactical and strategic wisdom accumulated over centuries of warfare, was not codified in treatises: there were no books to reflect upon, nor maps or diagrams to pore over. Like all ancient techniques, it was a wisdom that had crystallized and accrued around roles and functions. Just thought in action; knowledge fixed nowhere if not in a daily practice which continually improved upon, preserved, and handed it down through memory, observation, and example. For a long time, almost until its peak, the other unmatched Roman talent—for law—would also develop and be maintained in a not dissimilar condition.

It is possible Spartacus had a mentor; perhaps someone from among the Roman officers he would necessarily have known who spotted his qualities and offered guidance on a regular basis. But what can be taken for granted is that if we do not suppose an intense and enthusiastic military grounding, what happened later is incomprehensible.

Then came the split. Spartacus abandoned the imperial army—and with it the possibility of moving
up the social scale that loyal service would have
guaranteed—and became a deserter ("de milite, deser-
tor"). Again, we do not know why: a wrong suffered, a
private matter, a growing maturity of spirit? But some
conjectures can be made about the date and the location. There are those who believe Spartacus was already
in Italy in 83, having arrived with the five legions that
returned from the East with Sulla. If that is what happened, his desertion would have occurred in Italy,
where he would likewise have led his life as a "bandit"
prior to being captured. In this case, Spartacus would
have been a fugitive in the Peninsula twice: once, on his
own, sometime between the end of the eighties and the
first half of the seventies, and again—now in good
company!—in 73, which is the object of our story. But
this would have been a highly singular repetition, and
would undoubtedly have aroused the curiosity of the
ancient historians—and yet not a trace of it can be
found. At the same time, other clues (we will come to
these in a moment) point to Spartacus's presence in
Thrace after the eighties. I believe, then, that a different
reconstruction is preferable, which, if well-founded,
might also give us an idea of why he deserted.

Let's assume, then, that Spartacus did not come to
Italy with Sulla, but remained in Macedonia, and continued to fight in the imperial army (we know that at
least two legions did not return home). In 78 the Roman

troops still in the region were commanded by the pro-consul (he had been consul in 79) Appius Claudius Pulcher. In the winter of 77–76, he decided, although ill, to mount a campaign against some of the Thracian populations on the northern borders of the province. He marched north with all his available forces. Sparta-cus was one of his soldiers. Appius Claudius moved shrewdly, and had some successes. One of his aims was to suppress the Maidi, who had long been in re-volt. They were Spartacus's folk. The proconsul died in 76, in the theater of operations. Spartacus deserted. But instead of going into hiding, he probably carried on fighting, this time on the side of his own people. He became a rebel; for the Romans, a bandit (*latro*, accord-ing to the judgment reported by Florus). In reality he was a guerrilla fighter, a partisan.

It is just a conjecture: but it seems the only way to explain how Spartacus's conduct produced such con-trasting views, like the one recorded by Florus, and the other appraisal, almost certainly deriving from Sallust, picked up by Varro and not unknown to Plu-tarch, which, as we have seen, regarded him as blame-less and as having been unjustly enslaved. It is highly improbable that this latter view could have been based on an alternative version of the factual circumstances— his desertion and revolt, in a word, the backbone of the events recalled by Florus: who would have been able to gather and verify a different story, and how? And how would this tradition have formed? It makes better sense to think that the more favorable judgment rested on a moral evaluation, capable of overturning—in an extreme and polemical way—the thesis of "dishonor": an opinion that did not deny the facts, but gave them another meaning. Admittedly, Spartacus had deserted from the imperial forces, and placed himself beyond the bounds of Roman legality, but he had done so to avoid fighting his own people. This made him in a certain sense "blameless" (even though we can suppose there was a hint of provocativeness in the use of the word): emerging from his actions were, as it were, "ideological" motives, that someone like Sallust could well understand and perhaps even polemically justify.

Spartacus's time as a guerrilla was in any case short-lived. About it we know nothing, but it is easy to visualize a life of ambushes, of short, ferocious clashes, rapid retreats, and constant danger in a rugged terrain of forests, ravines, and mountains. We can imagine his thoughts as well—about Rome, his people, himself. And we would like—nor would it be out of place, given what we know about him (his Greek "gentleness")—to think of him, however far-fetched it might seem, in the company of a few books. At any rate it put the definitive seal on his warrior temperament—the crowning moment of his education.

The Roman repression was effective, and left few ways out. It is hard to conceive of Spartacus being free beyond 75. He was captured, probably in an ambush (this would explain why he was taken alive, without serious injuries), and immediately—as usually happened—sold as a slave. In those years Thrace was, together with Gaul, one of the principal catchment areas for the whole Roman slave system.

We can imagine a slave trader following in the wake of the army—there were lots of them—immediately sniffing a good opportunity. Spartacus must have been a physically powerful man, and perhaps word of his strength and courage was already circulating. He was, then, an important if not precious commodity, and it would have been a waste to dispatch him to the prison-quarters of a farm estate or plantation in Campania or Etruria. His future as a gladiator was already decided.

Once captured, the subsequent steps were determined by the routine of the imperial slave trade, and can readily be presumed: transferral (together with other similarly unfortunate companions) to a Macedonian port—Dyrrhachium or Apollonia—and from there a short sea voyage to Brundisium. Then, on foot, to Rome. That he ended up in the capital is recalled by Plutarch, and we have no reason to doubt it.

It was the only time Spartacus saw the heart of the empire. Of course, we do not know what his impressions were; he was almost certainly in chains, and quite unable to move. But in the preceding years, especially when serving in Sulla's army, everyone around him would have talked about Rome, and who can say how many times he had pictured it in his mind's eye: its enormous size, extraordinary wealth, the magnificence of its seats of power—the Capitoline Hill, or the Curia. And now, despite his unhappy state, he would have been able to take in some images, smells, and sounds, and to compare them with his earlier daydreams: the glimpse of a street, temple profile, or towering building; a teeming market or cluster of shops; the flavor of a soup or the stench of a steep alleyway packed with carts and people, together with the aroma of freshly baked bread or the scent of a garden.

· 7 ·

Spartacus was not alone in Rome. At his side, was his companion—a Thracian woman.

This figure emerges from obscurity on just one occasion, before being swallowed up again by darkness. It is Plutarch who mentions her, and who knows if he was still drawing on Sallust. We have no idea when, where, and how Spartacus met her—presumably after 80, and almost certainly in Macedonia or Thrace; it is unlikely to have happened in Italy, and this (as we have said) makes Spartacus's presence in those regions after 83 much more probable. The woman was a priestess, dedicated to making prophecies.

The Thracians had strong religious feelings rooted in mysteries with a potent magical and orgiastic core, barely tempered, in circles more receptive to the Greek influence, by a patina of Hellenization. According to one well-known theory, it was precisely from Thrace that the Greeks picked up the cult of Dionysius: a complex, intrinsically tragic deity expressing the unfathomable contradictoriness of life, who overturned fixed roles, inebriated minds, erased borders—between the living and the dead, the human and the animal, nature and culture—exalted reproductive functions, and considered women a privileged medium for an ecstatic relation with the supernatural. We now know that the hypothesis of the Thracian provenance of this figure is unfounded: its earliest origins were Minoan, and it was then transplanted to Attica. But a god with traits similar to the Greek Dionysius was undoubtedly an ancient and dominant presence in the religiosity of the Thracians, and fitted well with the ancient vocations of that people: war, wine, land, hunting.

Spartacus's companion—even her name is unknown to us—was consecrated to Dionysius: she was one of his bacchants. The bond with her man is thus tinted with mystic shades and implies a strong emotional involvement. Plutarch talks of her as being possessed by trances ("ton Dionyson orghiasmois")—situations in which female sexuality, completely transgressing the rules of everyday life, became a direct sign of the divinity, and the path to communion with it. It was all very familiar to the Roman ruling circles: around a century earlier they had issued a harsh senatorial decree to put a stop to the spread of these practices in the lower layers of society, well aware of their potentially subversive effects on the social order. A rigid disciplining of the female—of bodies no less than minds—lay in fact at the basis of the republican aristocratic ethic.

What happened, according to Plutarch, is this: "It is said that when he [Spartacus] was first brought to Rome to be sold [as a slave], a serpent was seen coiled about his face as he slept, and his wife, who was of the same people as Spartacus, a prophetess, and subject to visitations of the Dionysiac frenzy, declared it the sign of a great and terrifying force which would attend him to a[n] . . . issue." (And here the tradition of Plutarch's text lets us down: in some manuscripts the outcome is described as *atyches,* meaning "unfortunate," in others *eutyches,* that is, "fortunate," the exact opposite. From a stylistic point of view, the immediately preceding word, *phoberas*—which has negative connotations and should therefore be translated as "terrifying" rather than in a simply neutral manner—used in relation to Spartacus's force, would seem to point to a bleak end, suggesting a prophecy that foretold the worst. On the other hand, it must be said that a bright prediction would have given Spartacus an aura of predestination that was not at odds with the subsequent unfolding of events. And in any case, could not the mere fact that Spartacus managed, after touching rock bottom, to regain his liberty and to fight to the end with a weapon in hand be in itself considered a "fortunate" outcome?)

The Greek author is the only one to recall this episode, and we have no way of judging its reliability. We do not know where Spartacus was held in Rome, and hence whether the place was compatible with the presence of a snake (apart from anything else, ancient tales abound with "prophetic" snakes). That he was not alone is by no means implausible. It was not uncommon in trading practices for prisoners to be followed by their loved ones, even though we know much less about Roman female slavery than we would like to—and in our case the woman might quite easily have been captured together with Spartacus, having shared his life as a fugitive and guerrilla fighter. That she was also a priestess—and therefore of high standing among the

Thracians—is also credible, and would confirm that Spartacus's ties and roots were anything but humble.

That is as far as we can go. Perhaps the story was pure invention, sparked by the commonplace Roman view that a religious component lay at the origin of every slave revolt (we will come back to this): a simple strand of the Spartacus legend, formed who knows how, gathered by Sallust and then picked up by Plutarch. But in any case it is not without value for us. Based on reliable materials and circumstances, it enables us to link Spartacus to a profound aspect of the culture of the Thracian peoples, bringing out a third feature of his background, besides his Greek "gentleness" and his vocation for arms: that religiosity tinged with mysteries which must have been a decisive part of the inner life and precocious charismatic force of the young warrior, to whom it offered a potent reserve of will and determination.

How long did Spartacus spend in Rome? Certainly not long—a few weeks, a couple of months at the most: this was the normal pace of proceedings in the slave trade. Then he was sold again. The buyer was the Lentulus Batiatus we have already spoken of, the owner of the camp in Capua. How much he paid is unknown, but probably many thousands of sesterces—a considerable investment—if the average price of a nonspecialist slave in that period was around one to two thousand sesterces (a thousand was also the sum mentioned by Columella for the purchase, in Italy, of a *iugerum* of land suitable for growing vines), and if, in the first century A.D., a grammarian slave would fetch, albeit in an exceptional case, as much as seven hundred thousand sesterces.

As soon as he could, his new master sent him to Capua, along the Appian Way, probably together with other prisoners who may have been bought on the same occasion (slaves were often purchased in lots). His woman went with him. It was the middle of 74, or thereabouts.

· 8 ·

Once in Capua, Spartacus must have immediately started thinking of escape. As an expert in military matters, it would have taken no more than a glance to weigh up the level of security of his new prison, and to gauge his chances of getting out. We can imagine the living conditions were hard, but that the surveillance was not particularly tight. For certain, he was not always in chains. To fight in the arena, he had to be in good physical shape and, from his master's point of view, he needed above all to have some motivation to survive. That meant reasonable food (by the standards of the time), the possibility to train regularly, assistance from physicians and masseurs, the guarantee of a minimum of personal dignity, and above all, being able to keep his woman with him. He would have been instructed in the rules of the games, had opportunities to get to know others, glean information, and forge ties; probably to get an idea of the layout of the city and the local area, and perhaps of the size of the Roman garrisons outside the camp. There was also time, in the gladiators' daily routine, for barrack-room jokes and boasts, as we learn from graffiti found in Pompeii. In those months, Spartacus would certainly have fought in the arena: in Capua, perhaps in Pompeii, maybe in other cities in Campania, less probably in Rome. He must have won, and have killed. His fame would have grown.

The other prisoners were mainly Gauls and Thracians like himself. There were probably Germans as well. And it was with two Gallic gladiators, Crixus and Oenomaus, later his escape companions, that the plan for the revolt was hatched. We know nothing about them except for their name and origin (Oenomaus was probably just a stage name used in the arena). They were undoubtedly top-class fighters, possibly eminent members of their tribes of origin. And they must have exerted a powerful influence over the prisoners of their own people. Admittedly, they were from another culture to that of Spartacus, in all likelihood less Romanized, and with no Hellenistic influences. All they had in common was their prison routine and their profession of arms. What relations were like between the different ethnic groups in the Capua camp is unknown. There were major language barriers, and the custodians, it can readily be assumed, would not have encouraged interaction. Spartacus would have talked in Latin with the two Gallic chiefs—just as slaves belonging to different African peoples would communicate in English on plantations in the southern states of America before the Civil War.

The plan they devised was ambitious: not the flight of a small group, but a mass rebellion involving hundreds of prisoners (two hundred, according to Plutarch), possibly the entire population of the camp. From the outset, Spartacus was thinking big. We can imagine him driven by extreme determination, between one bout of combat and the next; his life could not end like that, in an arena, fighting as a gladiator. The gods—his Dionysius, who spoke through his woman—had foreseen other things for him.

It would certainly have taken months to build up such a vast network of conspirators in what were unfavorable conditions. There was, however, a betrayal, perhaps by one of the slaves in on the plot, possibly a guard who had offered complicity, or a local outside the prison with whom the inmates had dealings, and who was aware the plan: around concentrations of slaves, especially in the cities, webs of relations tended to form with the plebs living in the immediate vicinity. Sometimes there was even a certain mutual solidarity.

Whatever happened, the situation precipitated suddenly. With so many people involved, it was hard to keep the secret. About seventy slaves, no more than that (there is a slight discordance about the exact number), perhaps warned of the tip-off, managed to act in time and avoid the impending reprisal. They were unarmed and desperate: a horrendous death awaited them if they were taken. Occupying the kitchens, probably during the night, they armed themselves as best they could with roasting spits, staves, and butcher's knives.

Somehow they succeeded in overcoming the guards, without a doubt less expert and motivated than they were, and perhaps fewer in number as well. A dash to the gates and then they were out, into the darkness, before anything could be done to halt them. Together with Spartacus went his companion; if she had remained she would have been tortured and killed as an accomplice. And it is quite possible that she was not the only woman.

The escape had begun. No more than a year must have elapsed since Spartacus's arrival in Capua. It was no later than the spring of 73.

They immediately abandoned the city. There was only one way to go, and it can be assumed they had long since chosen it: southward, probably on a route parallel to the Via Annia, which led toward Nola and Nuceria. In the other direction lay the Appian Way and Rome, which would have taken them right into the arms of the enemy. Better to put as much distance as possible between them and the capital, and to head for territory with plenty of resources, where it would be easy to survive.

A stroke of luck helped them straight away. Quite by chance, they intercepted a stock of gladiators' arms destined for the camp of a nearby city, perhaps Pompeii, being shipped in a convoy of carts. The fugitives quickly seized them—they were already a step up on spits, sticks, and knives.

In Capua and the surrounding area there were no significant Roman garrisons at that moment. What would have been the purpose? Rome was developing an extraordinary talent for organizing the control of its territories, in Italy and abroad. It exploited to the full the self-interested loyalty of local ruling groups, and their rivalries as well, encouraging innocuous small-scale autonomies and bloodless competition, in order to hold vast spaces with a handful of men and a gossamer-thin web of administrative structures (Britain would do the same in India)—to say nothing of the limited demographic spread of the population in the ancient world, which facilitated this strategy to no small degree.

· 9 ·

The first troops that could be dispatched against the fugitives were a few units from the garrison in Capua, poorly trained and even more poorly commanded. There were no other forces nearby. The bulk of Roman strength was occupied in far-off lands, as we will see. And in any case the Roman administration and local officials probably believed nothing more was required to deal rapidly with a band of slaves.

It was the beginning of a long chain of errors and underestimations. The pursuers quite possibly tried to cut off the fugitives and halt their march southward. But the slaves, revived by their newfound freedom no less than by the first raids and the rich pickings to be had in the area, easily got the better of them. In this way they (finally!) managed to obtain some real battle weapons, taken from their dead or fleeing enemies. Plutarch recalls that it seemed a dream come true for fighters who were once again their own men to be able to ditch their gladiators' swords and shields, which "they cast aside contemptuously as dishonourable and barbarous." Again, the observation may originally have been Sallust's, designed to integrate as far as possible the Spartacus story into a narrative that somehow gave it a more complex meaning not limited to the servile origins of the revolt (Sallust was a democrat, at least in the ancient sense of the word, but this did not stop him embracing the idea that slavery lay outside the sphere of the genuinely human). The swapping of arms thus took on the significance of an intense ceremony, conducted "gladly" *(asmenoi):* a full-blown rite of passage from the arena to the battleground; a purification, a scraping away of the past, which restored, in their own eyes if not in those of the Romans, dignity to men who felt they had lost it, and transformed them from slaves into real warriors, as they had formerly been. It is no coincidence that their old circus weapons are described in the story as "barbarous": gladiatorship still had the ethnic associations characterizing its early period. Those who practiced it were not just slaves but also barbarians, at least in the minds of their masters. So the fugitives really were emerging from an abyss. It is not hard to imagine Spartacus at the center of the scene evoked by Plutarch. For him it was actually a kind of return to the past: he had already wielded Roman weapons, and was now being reunited with them.

In the first days of their march, after they had forced open the road to the south, the fugitives took over a fortified position. Exactly where is unclear, but it may have been between Capua and Nola. Here they stopped for a few days (or perhaps a little longer) and, according to Plutarch, took advantage of the respite to choose their leaders. He says there were three, and cites Spartacus as the "first" one, omitting the names of the other two; Appian, besides Spartacus, mentions Crixus and Oenomaus, describing them as "subordinate officers" *(ypostrategoi)*, while Florus and others (for example, Orosius) put all three on the same level. Whatever was really the case, the discordance clearly points to the existence of a problem in the ranks of the rebels, though overemphasized, as we shall see, by the Roman tradition: that of the command structure. Spartacus unquestionably had a charismatic power—by virtue of culture, military and perhaps even oratorical talents, and capacity of vision—superior to that of the others, which would have given him an indubitable preeminence. Such an advantage may conceivably have led to an explicit investiture; at any rate the ethnic diversity of the rebels made mediation indispensable, though far from easy, irrespective of whether a specific hierarchy was maintained. We will have occasion to return to this issue later.

There is no doubt that Rome was informed immediately of the revolt: news reached the capital fast—this too was part of the Roman imperial system. The consuls in 73 were Gaius Cassius Longinus (one of his descendants would become a famous jurist who dared to oppose Nero) and Marcus Terentius Varro Lucullus.

Sulla had died in 78, and the rising star in the Roman political firmament, Pompey, was in Spain with a special command.

It is likely that both the senate and the consuls had initially judged the garrison in Capua sufficient to hunt down the rebels. But having realized that this was not the case, they decided on direct intervention. Between four and six cohorts—about three thousand men, according to Plutarch—were sent from the capital, possibly led by one of the praetors of the year (though as we have said, there is uncertainty about the position). They were not crack troops, but a step up on the soldiers stationed in Capua. It took them just a few days to reach and close in on the rebels, who in the meantime had grown in number and were now several hundred strong. Other runaway slaves—an endemic phenomenon in the territories between Etruria and Campania—were beginning to join them, as were free men, probably shepherds who lived in the mountains, some already virtually as bandits.

Spartacus probably did not expect such a quick Roman reaction, and had reckoned on having more time to get organized. With a numerically superior enemy at his heels, he decided to move toward Vesuvius, where the terrain seemed more favorable for resistance. Local men would have helped him in the disengagement maneuver. He was, after all, accustomed to such tactics, and well versed in the operational protocols of the imperial forces. The Romans, for their part, believed they had him in their grasp, and could wrap the matter up immediately. They were sorely mistaken.

TWO

THE COMMANDER

· 1 ·

T HE rebels spent a few days in their newly won camp, where they found weapons, food, and a great deal else—the logistics of the Roman army never disappointed. Then they left Vesuvius, but not, at least for the moment, the Campania region. The theater of the following developments was still the area between Capua, Puteoli, Nola, Pompeii, Nuceria, and (perhaps) Beneventum.

Did they have a plan? And if so, when was it conceived?

It is hard to say. Spartacus must have had some sort of idea, probably roughed out while he was still in captivity, as subsequent events would seem to suggest. On the other hand, the strategic planning of military commanders in the ancient world—including Caesar's, the most advanced of them all—is not even remotely comparable to that of modern armies. Yet of two things we can be sure: Spartacus was not contemplating a hurried escape from the Peninsula, possibly back into Thrace, and nor was he envisaging a future as a solitary bandit in Italy, accompanied at the most by a small armed band. He certainly had good geographic information (this would emerge without question), and knew how to move on the ground. If he had been thinking of one of these solutions, he would have acted very differently. In the first case, speed would have been essential, as he must have been fully aware. Hanging around in Campania was not only pointless, but dangerous as well; instead, he would have had to head northeast as soon as possible, in the direction of the Adriatic (to find ships—but with whose help? After all, the Thracians were not exactly a seafaring people), or, more likely, toward the mountain passes of the Eastern Alps. At any rate, it would have been better to split up—each toward his own destiny.

In the second hypothesis—life as a bandit—he would have gone into hiding, disappeared, heading with his companion and a few trusted men in the direction of the nearest mountains—and there were plenty close at hand, between the Apennines and Abruzzi. Many fleeing slaves used to do just that. And in his situation, here too it would have been important not to stick together, but to break up into small groups, perhaps almost immediately, just outside Capua, and to vanish into the wild, sparsely populated territory.

Instead he kept all the fugitives together, running the risk of being spotted by Roman reconnaissance, and remained in Campania. What's more, he tried to augment his ranks, accepting as many new recruits as possible.

A conclusion must therefore be drawn: from the very beginning Spartacus had something different in mind, which prompted him to pursue a specific goal—to build an army and continue to fight. Florus writes that he and his men were not content just to have escaped. They wanted "revenge" as well. It is an evaluation that should not be neglected, though referring only to the desire for "vendetta" as the motivation for their actions appears to be a simplification of more complex feelings and states of mind. But certainly, once they had broken the siege on Vesuvius, it is evident that Spartacus and his companions were no longer just battling for their own immediate personal safety, but had more ambitious aspirations, in which fighting the Romans went beyond a mere question of survival.

In the space of a few weeks the men they could count on multiplied. Florus says over ten thousand soon gathered. And Appian and Plutarch, albeit in more general terms, also report a rapid growth in the rebel forces. Classical sources are to be treated with great caution when it comes to figures: we are in the ancient realm of the approximate, not the modern one of precision, and numbers were mentioned more to indicate tendencies that to report quantities exactly. Even glaring errors were considered acceptable provided they did not make nonsense of the facts. So what we have here is probably an exaggeration. But there was indisputably a significant enough increase to enable Spartacus, from then on, to face up to sizable Roman formations and to mount operations at least on a tactical scale. By now he undoubtedly had several thousand fighting men.

It was no longer an escape, it was a revolt.

We can reasonably suppose that the majority of the new followers were still slaves—Gauls, Thracians, Germans, perhaps some from the East. They are unlikely to have been casual arrivals: fugitives encountered on the way, as must have happened during the march toward Vesuvius in the days immediately after the breakout. This would not explain such a substantial rise in numbers in so brief a time. Instead we must think of something more like a recruitment campaign, conducted fairly systematically, and provoking insubordination and flight from the *villae* characterizing the Campanian agricultural settlements between Capua, Puteoli, Pompeii, and Nola. The density of slaves on these farms was at its peak, shaping the social fabric of the region's agrarian landscape. The increasing concentration of properties in the hands both of the municipal aristocracy and the senatorial nobility and equestrian ranks of the capital, which had been under way for quite some time, did not necessarily lead to the establishment of large agro-pastoral estates, or *latifundia*, at the expense of the intensive farming—vines, cereal crops, olives—practiced on the *villae*. The unification of different properties in the hands of a single owner frequently did not affect the operative autonomy of the preexisting units—and therefore the typology of the *villae*—where the now consolidated practice of rationally organized cultivation required a significant presence of slave laborers, often only loosely guarded in an attempt to reduce costs and increase profits.

At the beginning of the first century, tens of thousands of slaves must have been working in the rural areas of Campania, representing an obvious base of support to which the rebels could turn. Without necessarily imagining a general revolt, it is not hard to visualize a kind of insurrectional chain reaction as the news spread and columns of Spartacus's forces approached, ready to weigh in if required. The slaves of the *villae* were joined by slave-shepherds from the nearest mountains, "robust, agile people," according to Plutarch, from areas toward Samnium or the city of Nuceria, and on down to the sea—wild expanses of open woodland very different to the neat geometric parcels of land around the *villae*—or from *latifundia* given over to pasture or to extensive plantations. Ownership of sizable flocks was an undisputed mark of prestige, and as early as the second century servile labor had begun to be used heavily for large-scale livestock farming in the south. Nonurban Roman Italy was far from homogeneous in terms of production, social conditions, and material culture. As Andrea Giardina has noted, "the nature of places shaped human behavior and fixed ethnic types"; between mountains and banditry there was by now a close correlation, borne out on many occasions.

Finally, among Spartacus's new recruits, as we have already said, there were free men, also from the countryside ("eleutheroi ek tōn agrōn," Appian carefully specifies): a rural proletariat forced to work on a day-by-day basis in extremely hard conditions, veritable drifters ("men gathered together from everywhere," again according to Appian) ruined by long military *corvée* no less than by the widespread availability of cheaper slave labor, and pushed to the very limits of survival. The hapless condition of the peasants—once the backbone of the republic—was emerging as one of the crucial problems of Roman-Italic society between the second and first centuries: attempting to get on top of that disaster had been, fifty years earlier, the failed objective of the Gracchi. We cannot say how many joined Spartacus. Probably only a few, at least in this early phase, compared to the overall number of slaves—but it is a point to which we shall return.

· 2 ·

More troops were dispatched from Rome under the command of Publius Varinius, another of the praetors in 73 (remembered by Frontinus as proconsul, but this was almost certainly an oversight). As far as we know, he too had no significant military experience. The senate was probably beginning to realize the delicacy of the situation in Campania, and yet still hoped to handle matters without having to resort to special measures. No information is available about the initial size of Varinius's force, but we do know that he tried to strengthen it, as was usual in these cases, by recruiting during the march toward the enemy, between southern Latium and Campania. Presumably the route was once again the Appian Way. It is a singular coincidence that both Varinius and Spartacus boosted their numbers by drawing on the demographic resources of adjoining if not identical territories. In the conflict, though it continued to be viewed as a slave revolt, disturbing shadows were beginning to loom large, heralding more serious threats. On both sides, albeit not in a proportionate way, there were free men with common peasant origins—in Spartacus's ranks, a handful had probably even obtained Roman citizenship.

The praetor was assisted by two of his legates, Furius and Cossinius, about whom, apart from their names, we know virtually nothing (the former had been praetor in 75). The available accounts are extremely confused at this point, but we can piece together the sequence of events all the same.

Varinius decided to split his force, or at least not to wait for them to join up (if they had set out, as is possible, from different places and at different times) before engaging the enemy. He probably hoped to surround Spartacus, who had still not moved far from Vesuvius, and to close in from more than one direction. It was a rash maneuver, especially as he did not have well-trained soldiers, but for the most part recruits of dubious reliability. Spartacus himself might conceivably have induced the Roman commander to make this choice, leading him to believe he could be easily outflanked and caught in a pincer movement. The fact remains that the rebels immediately seized the opportunity to attack the Roman columns, dangerously far apart, separately, and with numerical supremacy.

They fell upon Furius's detachment, which was two thousand strong (according to Plutarch), and wiped it out, possibly in an ambush, and at any rate before the other Roman formation could converge on them. Then they moved quickly to face Cossinius, likewise in command of forces described by Plutarch as "sizable," which were nearer to the coast. Once again, Spartacus relied entirely on his capacity for initiative and tactical improvisation. Cossinius had halted his column at a *villa* near Salinae, close to the sea between Herculaneum and Pompeii. He may have been the guest of a landowner friend. His soldiers were camped in the vicinity, but the spot he had chosen for himself was undefended—a serious imprudence. The Roman commander was bathing (this detail is reported by Plutarch, who got it from Sallust), quite obliviously, when Spartacus's men—well informed of his whereabouts—were suddenly upon him. They took the *villa* and all his baggage. Cossinius barely managed to escape and reach his soldiers. But Spartacus followed in hot pursuit, and tore into his camp before he had time to collect himself. Once again surprise was complete, and the Romans routed. Many fell in battle—among them the incautious legate.

Varinius, with the bulk of the Roman troops, was not far away, probably a little to the northeast, between Nola and Herculaneum. It is possible that, to carry out the encirclement, he had attempted a three-pronged movement, with Cossinius on the coast, Furius in the center, and he himself, in strength, further to the left. But the plan had failed completely.

In the following weeks, Varinius clashed several times with Spartacus, and it is to one of these episodes—mentioned by Plutarch—that fragment 95 of Sallust's *Histories* (from the third book) must refer. In it is a description of the moments preceding the battle: "and so above all, as happens in the most extreme circumstances, everyone recalled their loved ones at home, and everyone, in each unit, made final preparations."

Actually, however, nothing decisive occurred. Spartacus managed each time to get the better of his opponent—as Plutarch once again recalls—while avoiding full engagement. And Varinius, for his part, had become cautious after the disasters that had befallen his lieutenants.

Autumn was now imminent, and both sides found themselves caught up in a difficult campaign of attrition—what's more in a fairly restricted area. In fragment 96, Sallust paints a vivid and realistic picture. The rebels did not have enough arms to equip all the new recruits, and were forced to temper wooden stakes in fire to use as lances. Food was also becoming scarce. But the Romans were not well placed either, partly due to the haste with which the army had been assembled: desertions and lack of discipline were compounded by the consequences of a fever epidemic that broke out in that "heavy autumn."

Varinius decided to send his quaestor Gaius Toranius to Rome to inform the consuls and senate of the difficulties he was encountering, and in the meantime, with four thousand men, managed to press in to within shouting distance of the rebels' advance positions. We do not know where exactly, but this time the Roman camp was well protected with a "rampart, ditch, and extensive earthworks": the lesson had been learnt, albeit at great cost. It is not clear how Spartacus's forces were deployed, or the nature of the terrain, but at any rate he decided to disengage. The tactical scenario was not to his advantage on this occasion. Short of food supplies, his men were continually forced to go on raiding missions, which broke up the formations and divided their ranks, exposing them to the risk of a Roman attack for which they would have been unprepared. So Spartacus came up with another stratagem, also destined to be taken as an example, recounted fully by Sallust in the long fragment 96, and then picked up, like the one about Vesuvius, by Frontinus.

On a shadowy night, after the second watch—and therefore before midnight—Spartacus's men abandoned their camp in absolute silence. A lone trumpeter remained on guard. The bodies of fallen companions were propped up on stakes in front of the gate, so anyone observing from a distance would take them for sentries. They also lit big fires to give the impression the camp was fully operative—while they themselves moved toward more inaccessible terrain. It was a variant on the Vesuvius ruse, employing surprise to slip away instead of to attack. And as in the earlier instance, the way it was achieved permits a realistic calculation of numbers. It is unthinkable that such an operation was conceived to disengage an army of ten thousand men: a force that size could not possibly have been extricated without the Romans discovering them. Yet we know the maneuver worked perfectly, a sign that the figures involved must have been relatively modest—perhaps even less than half the number indicated by Florus.

It was not until full daylight that the Romans got wind of the trick. Made suspicious by the absence of sounds and the customary shouts of abuse from the enemy camp, Varinius sent out a detachment of cavalry to reconnoiter, and from a nearby hill they finally realized what had happened (but if it was a dominant position, why had the Roman commander not thought of occupying it previously?).

By then Spartacus was long gone, though in what direction we do not know (unfortunately there is a gap in Sallust's text at precisely this point). Certainly he was making for a mountainous area—possibly toward Nuceria, perhaps Samnium. Varinius did not follow him; he feared a trap, and pulled back cautiously to Cumae, just north of Naples, hoping to find fresh recruits. But he only spent a few days there before deciding to get back on the march again and to reestablish contact with the enemy, which in the meantime must have moved closer. Sallust is severe in his judgment of this choice: Varinius had nothing other than poorly trained, undisciplined, and combat-shy soldiers; taking them back into battle was, in his view, a rash decision. But Spartacus probably left the Romans no alternative. The disengagement had been merely tactical, to wriggle out of an unfavorable situation on the ground, but his aim was nonetheless to keep pressing Varinius, otherwise the rebels would not have been located so easily by Roman scouts after their successful deception.

Was Spartacus thinking of committing immediately to a pitched battle, or did he want to keep wearing down the enemy? Sallust reports a first disagreement on this issue among the rebel commanders, the foretaste of a still more radical and, in his reconstruction, decisive dissent which he went on to describe in the first part of fragment 98. Crixus, with the Gauls and Germans, were apparently in favor of the first option (nothing more is said about Oenomaus; perhaps he had been killed in an early clash, or maybe he had gone his own way with a small group of companions). Spartacus, on the other hand, seems to have had another plan, though we do not know what it was because Sallust's account—our only source on the matter—is once again interrupted at this point.

But the problem does not just lie in the textual lacuna. How did Sallust know about this hypothetical controversy between the leaders of the revolt? That he had firsthand testimony (accounts or memories originating directly from the rebel camp, in writing or through oral tradition) is simply not credible. The repression following the war erased everything. All he could do was draw on information gathered by Roman officers during operations and then incorporated into the most accredited version of the campaign (there were neither bulletins from the high command nor army archives in those days). But how had the Romans come by it? Only through prisoners or deserters—

ambiguous and not always reliable sources. Unless of course we are to believe they had inferred it from simple observation of the enemy's behavior in the field: confused or contradictory actions could have been interpreted as an unequivocal sign of internal division.

As can be seen, the channels of information are shaky, and require prudent evaluation. Nor should it be ruled out that Sallust exaggerated a little so as to make Spartacus stand out from the context of the revolt, both in order to respect the reality of the facts and for literary purposes. Ancient historians were extremely attentive to the stylistic effects of their writing, in which the search for aesthetic results was interwoven in a complex fashion with the strict pursuit of veracity. And the theme of discord among the rebels would prove (as we will see) to be a full-blown *topos* in the Roman narration of events.

At any rate, a battle did arrive fairly soon, in that same autumn—and Spartacus, whatever view he might previously have held, unquestionably played a leading role. For the Romans it brought further defeat. We do not know where the clash occurred—perhaps not far from Nola—or what course it took: Sallust's account of what happened has been completely lost. Varinius was lucky to survive, and only narrowly escaped being taken prisoner himself, but his force was routed. In the disaster, the lictors—attendants to consuls and praetors—were captured, as were the symbols of command, the *fasces,* which it was their duty to exhibit, and Varinius even lost his horse, as we learn from Florus, Plutarch, and Appian. Immediately afterward,

Toranius, who was probably coming to the praetor's aid with fresh troops, was also defeated.

The campaign of 73 was over.

· 3 ·

What did Spartacus have in mind now? The Roman tradition, gathered by Plutarch and Appian, recounts that after the victory he was inclined to leave Italy in order to return to Thrace, but that his view did not prevail among the rebels.

I believe this to be pure invention, and that Spartacus had never thought of doing anything of the kind.

It is the ascertainable facts—and nothing other than the facts, in their logical and historical connection—that makes this version implausible.

We have already said that if Spartacus had decided from the outset to go back to Thrace, he could have attempted it immediately after the breakout, and with a not inconsiderable chance of success. Some of his companions may have done just that. Staying put in Campania and gathering around him a small army of local rebels would certainly not have been any help in an escape, which required a quite different approach—speed, small numbers, covering tracks, and disappearing into the wide open spaces of the Peninsula, heading immediately north or, possibly, toward the Adriatic.

But let's just suppose that he came round to the idea of leaving Italy at some later point, for instance in the long, difficult autumn of 73. Well, what better occasion could there have been than after the defeat of Varinius? No Roman army in the vicinity, roads wide open in every direction, and, with winter drawing in, it would be like that for months. Who could stop him? Not all of his group, seemingly—and we will say more in a moment—would have followed him. But what did that matter? He would in any case, if he had wanted to abandon Italy, have had to break the ranks. Thracians, Gauls, and Germans would have gone in different directions—the way home was not the same for everyone. And that is without repeating that, to get out of the Peninsula, keeping the whole force together would have been not only pointless, but counterproductive. What sense did it make to take thousands of men to Thrace or Gaul—and to do what, once they had arrived? To carry on fighting the Romans from the borders, replicating, after a fashion, the Iberian experience of Sertorius? If that was the aim, he might just as well remain in the heart of the empire.

The truth is that Spartacus never thought of escaping from Italy: nothing about his conduct, on the basis of what we know, authorizes such a belief. The idea of the return home is a Roman overlay, probably invented by Sallust—or at any rate strongly reworked by him—and used in his reconstruction of Spartacus as a "character," which must have emerged powerfully in the design of the *Histories:* a valiant and "blameless" warrior (recalling Varro), forced to fight the Romans out of sheer necessity, whose desperate subversive courage would reveal the political and social fragility of the republic, but who had nothing in mind other than memories of his native land. The "return" motif formed part, what's more, of the stereotype of the fugitive slave and his intentions, as had been taking shape in an already long literary tradition. Ultimately, Spartacus was simply being labeled with a commonplace.

The opening of fragment 98 is devoted entirely to an account of the dissent that supposedly broke out in the rebel camp. Actually, the text, insofar as it can be read, does not talk explicitly about a return to Thrace—but the manuscript is in a very poor state and demands constant conjectural emendation, not all of which is immediately obvious. According to Sallust, Spartacus feared that by moving in a disorderly fashion, as they were doing, his men could be cut off and massacred, making it necessary "to leave as quickly as possible" (but in what direction is not said). It was a concern the historian had already attributed to the rebels during the long series of skirmishes with Varinius: that they might be surprised by the Romans—exposed and not in formation—while engaged in one of their frequent foraging raids, indispensable for procuring provisions. In the very brief fragment 97, mention is made of precisely such a raid, on Abella, a small town northeast of Nola, where the rebels clashed with local settlers trying to prevent their fields from being plundered. And it is likely that the devastation of Nola itself and of Nuceria, reported by Florus, must likewise be dated to the weeks immediately following the defeat of Varinius.

But Spartacus's opinion was not heeded by his companions. Sallust claims it was shared only by a few men "of foresight, of free and noble spirit." The others, "stupidly relying on the reinforcements pouring in [and here in any case emerges the crucial theme of recruitment and the necessity to extend the revolt] and on their own fighting qualities, or dishonorably unmindful of their country" (the only mention of the motif of the return), or "governed by their servile nature, sought for the most part nothing more than booty and the opportunity to indulge their cruelty."

At this point there is another break in the fragment of the *Histories*, and when the story resumes, the mood seems to have changed. An agreement has been reached. Spartacus invites his men to "go out into more open country, particularly grazing lands, where they could increase their number with select recruits before Varinius arrived with a new army." Here, finally, is Spartacus's real plan, emerging not through improbable direct sources, but deducible from the conduct of the rebel leader himself, and from the ensuing events: to retreat from Campania in order to find a more favorable theater of operations, where it would be easier to maneuver, secure provisions, and do further recruiting in order to face up to the inevitable return, in force, of the Romans. If there really was a dispute between the rebel leaders—let's say between Spartacus and Crixus—it would have concerned what tactics to adopt in the field, not the idea of leaving Italy. This is the truth—escape and Thrace had nothing to do with it! Spartacus was just looking for the most advantageous conditions in which to prepare for the campaign in the following spring.

We must imagine, then, that in Sallust's original account, the description of Spartacus's genuine objective—to head south and build up his fighting strength—was overlaid, with a compositional skill we are unable to appreciate due to the gaps in the text, by the theme of the "return home." The idea was probably to somehow play down the figure of the rebel commander in the eyes of Roman readers, setting his war against a background of familiar feelings and states of mind shaped by nothing other than love and nostalgia for a distant homeland.

But that is not how things stood. Instead, it was the magnetic pull of a wholly accepted predestination, and of a binding prophesy to respect—the mystic core of his mystery-cult beliefs—which dominated and guided Spartacus's choices, making up the emotional background of his military thinking and political calculations; besides, that is, the proud will to test his talent for command and to take on the owners of the world. He was not a man in flight. He had a destiny to fulfill, chosen by his god. Indeed, terrible prophecies had already been circulating between the East and West about the fall of Rome at the hands of "Asiatic" commanders. One had been related, in a period quite close to that of Hannibal, by Antisthenes of Rhodes: "I see the passing of bronze-chested forces from Asia, and kings joining together, and peoples of every kind against Europe [which here means Rome], and the din of horses, and the sound of lances, and a bloody massacre, and a terrible sacking, and the destruction of towers and leveling of walls, and unspeakable devastation." This was the stuff of Spartacus's dreams, the fabric of his imagination.

· 4 ·

To reinforce his ranks he had no choice for now but to go way south—and that is what he did. A good guide, a prisoner from the countryside to the south of Salernum, was found and the march commenced.

From Nuceria, already captured, they headed toward the Picentini Mountains, through Hirpinia, negotiating passes and forests, narrow gorges and streams swollen into rivers by the rain, trying all the time to avoid detection by the network of Roman scouts. At the beginning they probably kept away from the Via Annia. They crossed the mountains around Eburum (Eboli) and forded the River Sele, soon reaching, without being discovered, Nares Lucanae. Here, at dawn, following a night march, they swooped upon the small town of Forum Anni—a farming settlement north of the "Atinas Campus" area in the far south of today's province of Salerno—"surprising the peasants." Once again, the dynamic of the events suggests small groups sweeping forward in fast, coordinated movements rather than the measured advance of larger units. They may have split up and agreed to rendezvous at their destination in the heart of Lucania.

The autumn wheat was ripe in the fields. The rebels felt safe, and were probably tired after the long trek. Casting aside all restraint, they ran amok in a sudden outburst of violence—bloodshed, torture, burning, and rape. The local slaves, possibly tipped off about their arrival, sided with them en masse in a more or less spontaneous insurrection of a kind that had already occurred elsewhere—bonds and solidarity formed in an instant. It was they who led Spartacus's men to hastily concealed provisions and belongings, and pointed out the hiding places of their terrified masters. Power relationships fixed by the unremitting exercise of physical force dissolved instantly. Nothing seemed excessive or inviolable in the fury of the uprising—"barbarous rage and a servile nature" combined, Sallust writes coldly.

Spartacus, however, did not participate in the frenzy. In vain, he did everything he could—pleading even—to halt the massacre and to wrench his men out of a terrible spiral of "hatred." In the writing of the *Histories* his figure once more stands out alone against the backdrop of his companions—a leader, but a leader in solitude.

How much truth and how much literary construction there is in this account is again hard to say. Without a doubt, in Sallust's time a whole Italic—above all southern—tradition about the cruelty and violence perpetrated by the rebels in their forays was still alive, and it is quite feasible that what happened at Forum Anni rightly formed part of this reliable body of memories. But also Spartacus's aloofness from the conduct of his men, undoubtedly accentuated by Sallust, is not improbable either. We are told by Appian that the rebel chief often tried to impose a form of behavior which, though realistically accepting the harsh realities of war, prevented his men from becoming unbridled booty hunters—brigands without rules or scruples. It is information we have no reason to doubt—nobody had anything to gain from inventing it—and deserves to be judged with care. Spartacus always "divided the plunder in equal parts" (a policy which, according to Appian, made recruiting easier). What's more, "he prohibited the bringing in of gold or silver by merchants [into his camps], and would not allow his own men to acquire any: they only bought iron and bronze at great expense, without harming the merchants." The detail is reported by Pliny as well, which suggests he and Appian drew on the same source: probably Sallust (and Varro), but perhaps we should not exclude Posidonius.

Where did Spartacus get these models of behavior? We should look in various directions, toward more learned influences, which might have reached him from Greek democratic extremism and the economic egalitarianism that had long been spreading on the edges of that tradition, or even to the condemnation of the corrupting role of wealth found in significant strands of important philosophies (Stoicism, Cynicism), which might not have been unknown to him. Or, more simply, to basic notions of primitive rural communitarianism perhaps inherited from the customs of his own Thracian stock. Or, again—and this may be the most likely hypothesis—to a heterogeneous mix of overlapping cultural elements: doctrinaire ideas and popular reminiscences. Without forgetting that even bands of *latrones* often set rules for themselves. But in any case, I think it is less important to choose between these possible origins than it is to grasp what I would describe as the political-pedagogical aspect of Spartacus's conduct, whatever its provenance.

He did not simply want to raise an army to fight Rome and to leave a swathe of destruction in his wake. He wanted to give his troops instruction in a severe and rigorous discipline capable, in his judgment, not only of binding them together more effectively and honing their combat spirit, but also of sending a political signal. A message that alluded quite unequivocally—in the heart of the empire and during what, as we shall see, was a dramatic moment for its destiny—to the communitarian and subversive value (with respect to the constituted order) of a radical economic leveling, and to the rejection of the corrupting power of wealth and acquisitive greed. And this in the face of a society that was making money and opulence the measure of the world ("in Rome everything is for sale," Sallust would write not long afterward in relation to something else). It was neither compassion for the victims, nor a moral imperative that prompted Spartacus to "beg" his men to stop performing acts of pitiless cruelty in the tragic episode of Forum Anni. Rather, he was trying not to tarnish an image he hoped would become a symbol and a rallying cry—and seemingly it did, if, as Appian writes, Spartacus's egalitarian behavior was a determining factor in the unexpected success of his recruitment drive.

The force of that message—at once a program and an announcement—has reached us so toned down as to be almost completely obscured. The Roman repression, no less than the unfortunate loss of Sallust's *Histories,* literally removed it from sight. It is all the more precious, then, to be able to recover at least a distant echo. It renders even less credible the theory that Spartacus was set on returning to Thrace: Why train an army in this way if the only objective was escape? And it also sheds light on an essential aspect of his ambitions. He did not just want to be a commander; he wanted, however confusedly, to be a prophet, but a prophet armed to the teeth.

· 5 ·

The rebels remained in Forum Anni for another day and a night. Then they moved out, possibly continuing to avoid the Via Annia, and camped not far away "in a fairly spacious level area" that we are unable to pinpoint—it might have been near Grumentum—putting the local settlers to flight. Spartacus was by now the master of Lucania. He had greatly increased his fighting strength, as he had hoped. Sallust reports that he doubled his forces after the Forum Anni episode alone. The new arrivals must for the most part have been slaves who had fled from their masters and their tasks as shepherds or farm laborers. But we cannot exclude that, as before, a certain number of free men joined him as well—and this time they would not just have been brigands. A former slave whose name has been saved by Sallust, Publipor, who knew the terrain like the back of his hand, served as their guide.

And yet, even though there were no sizable Roman garrisons in the area, the inhabitants of the entire region remained on the whole hostile—terrorized but inimical: "the only place which would be safe for them would be that in which they had established a fortified position," we read in Sallust. Of course, the judgment might not be objective. But the fact remains that there are no reports, in those circumstances, of anti-Roman revolts.

In rapid succession, Spartacus took two cities on the Ionian coast, Thurii and Metapontum. With a splendid Greek past, they were of some strategic importance as well, albeit already in decline. But in both cases they had to be taken by force, and their capture was accompanied by wanton bloodshed and devastation, with "terrible destruction," writes Florus. The rebel army never managed to forge ties with significant sections of local populations, except perhaps around Thurii (as would emerge later), nor were the captured towns ever held. We cannot say whether or not an attempt was made to do so. In any case it continued—was constrained—to act like an army on the move, maneuvering in enemy territory.

At any rate, Lucania was a good place to spend the winter: a mild climate, the Roman troops a safe distance away, the bountiful Sibari Plain close to hand, abundant supplies. From the nearby seas—the Ionian and the southern Tyrrhenian—there must have arrived, with news and merchandise, traders eager to sell pretty much anything and pirates willing to show solidarity, attracted by what was happening—news soon spread across the Roman seas and this was the golden age for Mediterranean piracy. After turbulent months, Spartacus could rest up and take stock, reorganize his ranks, continue to recruit new forces with less hurry, and plan his next moves. He was free once again, his own master, like in Thrace. And it is likely that his woman was still with him—perhaps, in the winter, they might also have conceived a child. We know nothing about this, but ancient demographic patterns lend credence to the idea.

· 6 ·

It was not the first time Rome had faced slave revolts. As early as the second century, imperial expansion had resulted in the establishment of a full-fledged Mediterranean slave system, with the concentration in Italy—both in the cities and the countryside—of unprecedented numbers of prisoners. We are talking, in Spartacus's time, of millions of men and women: probably between two and three in the Italic Peninsula and in Sicily—about a third of the overall number of inhabitants. The proportions were not the same in the rest of the empire, but in the mining centers of Greece and Spain, or in the large coastal cities, they would not have been much less. For the most part, the slaves were first generation, deported after the wars of conquests, though we should not underestimate the size of the slave population born in captivity, the outcome of a not entirely negative demographic balance, notwithstanding often terrible living conditions.

Chattel slavery (the practice whereby slaves could be bought or sold without limit like any other goods, or as animals, "talking instruments," according to the definition of Varro, who was drawing on an Aristotelian motif) had spread to Rome relatively late, not before the third century. In more ancient times, there had just been a domestic kind of slavery, with a few slaves integrated into family structures and subjected to the same powers the head of the family had over his children.

When the new form began to be adopted, it immediately proved a resounding success, which soon eclipsed the example of every other ancient slave society, including classical Athens, where it had taken root at least as early as the fifth century. (Before then, various slave practices, often less invasive and violent than chattel slavery, had already existed for centuries in the Mesopotamian and Egyptian worlds, and in Greek society itself, without however ever acquiring such an essential function.)

The reasons for this rapid and overwhelming success lie above all in what turned out to be a decisive coincidence. The victorious wars, the result of an extraordinarily effective military machine, had opened up immeasurably vast spaces for the Roman conquerors, from the Po Plain to Sicily, not to mention Africa and Spain. But the endless succession of campaigns and the consequences of the war routine on the accumulation of growing wealth and its increasingly unequal distribution (due both to the outburst of a previously unknown aristocratic arrogance and to the unscrupulous acquisitiveness of the new merchant ranks) had produced an unexpected outcome. They had led to the social ruin (and political enfeeblement) of the broad Roman-Italic strata of small landowning farmers whose compactness had until then constituted the vital strength of the republican armies, by preventing them from gathering the economic fruits of their victories and sacrifices. It was in some ways a paradoxical situation, described perfectly by Tiberius Gracchus in the seventh decade of the second century, as recounted by Plutarch: " 'The wild beasts that roam over Italy,' he said, 'have every one of them a cave or lair to lurk in; but the men who fight and die for Italy have nothing but air and light; . . . they fight and die to support others in wealth and luxury, and though they are styled masters of the world, they have not a single clod of earth that is their own.' "

It is credible that the crisis also had a significant demographic component, besides the well-known one of the uprooting of the rural population and the drift toward the cities. At any rate, the lands conquered by the Romans soon proved to be dramatically empty, and faced a structural need for cheap labor, which the progressive concentration of property in groups of *villae* with a single owner or in the nascent system of *latifundia* rendered even more acute—from Campania to Etruria to Sicily.

But in those same years, wars and trade were also giving rise to an unprecedented abundance of slaves: a virtually unlimited workforce, easily transportable by sea from one region of the empire to another. And so a fatal and irresistible combination kicked in between the demand for labor and the supply of prisoners. Of course, neither the conquering generals, nor the bold, unscrupulous pirates, nor the astute slaver traders had invented the new pattern of agriculture. It was the result, at first entirely independent, of another series of events—political, social, military. In a sense, one might also say that the demand had historically preceded the supply. And yet, at least from the middle of the second century, slavery alone underpinned, in Italy, the most efficient part of the whole economic fabric, characterized by an agrarian landscape where by now, again according to Tiberius Gracchus as related by Plutarch, " 'those who worked the land or tended to the flocks . . . were imported barbarian slaves' ": the same people who, Diodorus writes, were bought in "whole slave marts."

It was through just such country that Spartacus was moving.

· 7 ·

The presence of large numbers of slaves in great expanses of varied terrain posed problems of control and security that no ancient power had had to deal with until then. But without this great mass of forced labor (in agriculture, workshops, and services), Roman civic life—its culture and urban organization, politics and administration—would not have been as we have come to know it. The relationship between slavery and civilization was perceived as one of necessity and sheer common sense in the imperial world. In the mindset of the dominant elites, slavery had become by far the most prevalent paradigm of wealth-generating manual labor. Production meant production by means of slaves. Any type of dependent work was sucked into the dark sphere of an almost total analogical assimilation with the servile condition, to the point that any contact between nature and organized human labor—the physical and social space, in the countryside and in workshops, where the vast majority of wealth destined for markets and not for self-consumption was created—appeared to be nothing other than a dead zone of human civilization, degraded by the abjectness of the servile state; a dark side of social life to be accepted as an elementary and immutable necessity, but which it would be quite pointless to look to for any higher form of thought.

Rome's commercial development—the imperial economic "miracle," with performance levels that would remain unequaled until the dawn of modernity—thus relied almost entirely on the working capacity of the slaves. But the more the system grew, the more the latter ended up paying the price. The reification of bodies—often branded with fire like ceramics or cattle—was accompanied by an annihilating pressure that no economic rationality could fully explain. Frequently it was due simply to a lack of measure and to a relentlessness on the part of the masters, springing from a mechanism of exploitation and dominion which, on that scale, was unprecedented and had no ethical or social points of reference. Nothing like it had ever existed until then.

It was in this way that the Mediterranean became not only a sea of commodities and markets, but also a sea of slaves, commodities themselves just like any other—and for a period of time, of slaves in revolt.

The crucial phase, when it really did seem as if something might crack, fell in the seven decades between 140 and 70. Spartacus represented at once its epilogue and its most critical point. It was the sign that an obscure threshold—also from a purely quantitative point of view—had been reached in the relations of dominion over the slave masses, not to mention the behavior of the masters, in that dramatic season in which it seemed as if anything could happen.

The first episodes of revolt, however, had taken place earlier—they can be dated to the beginning of the second century—and were carefully recorded by Livy—in Setia and in Praeneste, near Rome, in 198, when the praetor Lucius Cornelius Merula put five hundred rebel slaves, almost all Carthaginian prisoners (the Second Punic War had just finished), to the sword. Then, in Etruria, in 196, where the repression was led by the praetor Marcus Acilius Glaber, and soon after, in Apulia, in 185, among the shepherd-slaves of the *latifundia* (seven thousand were deemed guilty, and many were executed).

In this last case the Roman reaction also revealed another vein of disquiet. In Livy's account, many aspects of the insurrection are unclear, and it is quite probable that what happened was related to the sudden criminalization of the Dionysian cults already widespread in the capital (the last wave had perhaps arrived from Campania), and harshly punished with the senatusconsult "de bacchanalibus" of 186 (*bacchanalia* is the Latin word for "Dionysian orgies"). It was a moment of great tension in the history of the aristocracy's control of the masses, in which the ruling groups tried to stem the now irreversible disintegration of the city's ancient religion and its theological framework, and to channel in a less dangerous direction (for the constituted order) widely shared emotional needs that no longer had anything to do with the old rural world.

Now there is good reason to believe that the rebel shepherd-slaves of Apulia were associated with the cult of Dionysius and its destabilizing raptures, and that the Roman intervention was intended to quash both servile rebelliousness and religious subversion. If so, we would be in the presence of the first link, in the history of Rome, between rebel slave culture and Dionysian religiosity—a core of emotions and desires crystallizing around an ambiguous but potent message of liberation and subversion, capable of spreading from the lowest and most marginalized strands of society to the slave world itself. There can be no doubt, in fact, that the slaves in revolt were ethnically integrated into the local populations, and this made them more dangerous. Spartacus's priestess companion would in this case have reaffirmed such a tie, and she would have done so in a particularly suggestive way, given that, like Spartacus, she came from Thrace, where Dionysius was, in a certain sense, the "national" god.

It would not however be until about half a century after the rebellion in Apulia that a real qualitative leap took place in the scale and significance of insurrections: the years of the destruction of Carthage and Corinth, the repression in Numantia, the annexation of Pergamon—in which the expansionistic policy of the republic, by now impossible to justify on defense grounds, definitively acquired the features of a world dominion. Besides, mass rebellions were only the most extreme form of servile resistance to the violence of the masters. More immediate and direct ways included sly inobservance (bordering on sabotage) of orders received, or solitary flight (a fugitive slave was not distinguishable from a free man, and there was no personal identification in that age). Such phenomena were endemic, an inherent part of the social landscape of the epoch, and the comedies of Plautus and many passages in the correspondence of Cicero (who suffered to no small degree for the escape of the invaluable— and, we must presume, highly educated—slave in charge of his personal library) offer vivid testimony.

· 8 ·

Since 140 Sicily had been rife with bands of rebel slaves, who, with a motley albeit threatening array of weapons, plundered and destroyed whatever they came across. When they were still shepherds, they had been no worse: "The herdsmen, however, because of their experience of living outdoors and their military accoutrements, were high-spirited and overbearing; armed with clubs or spears or stout staves, and clad with the skins of wolves or wild boars, they made a terrifying sight and almost appeared equipped for war." It is a portrait of lawless brigands. Many of Spartacus's recruits who joined him between Lucania and Hirpinia must have resembled them.

But it was only in 135 that the rebellion exploded in Sicily on a mass scale and with a previously unseen degree of violence. "There was never a sedition of slaves so great," Diodorus writes. "Without a word of summons tens of thousands of slaves joined forces to destroy their masters," to the point that "all the island was in danger of falling into rebel hands."

According to Diodorus, a historian of no great talent active in the years between Caesar and Augustus, whose fragments from books XXIV–XXVI of his *Library* are our best source for reconstructing these events, the causes of the revolt could be traced back to two elements: the concentration, in Sicily, of large masses of prisoners ("an immense number" that "inundated" the island), and the inhuman cruelty with which they were treated by their masters. Quantity and discipline: the key points of the system. It is highly probable that the interpretation was substantially that of Posidonius; much less certain is the influence of Caecilius of Caleacte, a contemporary of Diodorus, a former slave who became a master of rhetoric, and the author of a work on the slave wars about which we know almost nothing.

The overall pattern of Sicilian agrarian history in the Roman age seems to confirm both these features: the great concentration of slaves and the aggressiveness and reckless disregard of the Roman masters dotted around the island. And it is also possible—though it cannot be verified with any certainty—that the Sicilian uprisings were linked in some measure to other insurrections of slaves that exploded at the same time in Asia Minor, in Attica, on Delos, even in Rome itself, where 150 prisoners hatched a conspiracy and tried to organize a revolt. The imperial communications system often relied on slave messengers, and it is quite feasible that news of the rebellions spread great distances to other groupings of slaves, who in turn propagated it in an ever-wider radius.

The information available to us relates above all to the beginning of the events, and it is hard to evaluate to what extent they were just the sign of widespread resistance by the slaves (almost all first generation) to being crushed by the mechanisms of exploitation and degradation, or how much they revealed a broader and more profound social instability on the island, to the point of rendering credible the image of a whole province in revolt against Roman domination. It is certain, though, that at least some of the lower orders became actively involved in the unrest. Diodorus writes:

> Many serious troubles befell the Sicilians. Yet the common people were not only unsympathetic, but actually gloated over their plight. Popular hatred was fueled by the inequality in their respective lots, and the disparity in their modes of life. And their envy, from being a gnawing canker, turned to joy at the sight of the ruinous state into which the privileged had fallen, reduced to a condition they had formerly despised. The worst thing was that, while the rebels, making prudent provision for the future, did not set fire to the country estates nor damage

the stock or the stored harvests, and abstained from harming anyone engaged in agriculture, the populace, using the slave revolt as a pretext, made sallies into the country and with the malice of envy not only plundered the estates but set fire to the buildings as well.

This is the description, not of an alliance, but of a contiguity of insubordination and rejection, a sort of parallel rebelliousness, where the slaves—who in any case (as we shall see) tried to establish some kind of alternative order to the ferocity of their masters—proved to be more responsible and far-sighted.

At any rate the rebels, among whom an oriental ethnic component prevailed—almost all the Sicilian slaves came from the eastern Mediterranean—captured a number of important fortified cities: Henna (now Enna), which they made their capital, and then Agrigentum (Agregento) and Tauromenium (Taormina). From among their own they chose a king, Eunus, a "Syrian" born in Apameia (though the adjective was often used for all slaves of oriental origin). Diodorus presents him as a coward and a charlatan, who resorted to underhand tricks in order to pass himself off as a prophet and a magician in direct contact with his deity, a Syrian goddess named Atargatis, who was associated with the mystery cult of the Magna Mater, which had been gaining ground, amidst great popular expectations, in Rome since 191. And yet, despite this judgment, Eunus really must have exerted a remarkable influence, given that he was able to rapidly unify under his command the two branches of the revolt, in the eastern and then the western part of the island, where the rebels were led by a former slave from Cilicia, Cleon, who proved to be both brave and audacious.

What emerges once again from Diodorus's account is the relationship between mystery cults and slave rebellion, a common thread running through the whole cycle of the great revolts. The rebel slaves—Thracians, Gauls, Germans, or Easterners—always turned out to be hungry for the supernatural, in search of emotional experiences and forms of belief able to touch a chord in the depths of their inner life and to compensate them for the systematic annihilation of their personality in captivity. "All this time the poor slaves may not move their lips, even to speak. The slightest murmur is repressed by the rod; even a chance sound—a cough, a sneeze, or a hiccup—is visited with the lash. There is a grievous penalty for the slightest breech of silence. All night long they must stand about, hungry and dumb."

Another important element is also recorded in Diodorus. The rebels on the island immediately tried to organize themselves politically, attempting to set up, in the "liberated" territory, something resembling a Hellenistic monarchy, a Seleucid kingdom (we must imagine, bearing in mind Eunus's homeland) transposed into the heart of Sicily. They even minted their own coins. This aspect makes the revolt comparable in some ways to episodes of resistance typically associated with modern colonial slavery, in which the rebels established stable communities of ex-deportees that eluded, for more or less prolonged periods of time, the laws of their masters: the cases of so-called marronage— not infrequent in America, from Brazil to Jamaica, in the seventeenth and eighteenth centuries—which sometimes ended up involving thousands of fugitives. In the Mediterranean of the third century, something not dissimilar had already happened in Chios, though only there, in the mountains of the island, as we learn from Athenaeus.

But in the winter of 73–72, when the Roman armies were far away and he was effectively the master of Lucania, Spartacus did not try to build anything of the kind. He made no effort to give the revolt a settled character and a territorial rootedness. The cities that fell into his hands were sacked and then immediately abandoned, and he never attempted in any stable fashion to impose his authority—we might even say sovereignty—on a circumscribed geographic space, not even the area between Bruttium and Lucania. Perhaps he did not yet feel ready for such a step. He also might not have been encouraged by the behavior of the local populations. But in any case he acted for now as the chief of an army operating in enemy territory, not as the founder of a political community. Even when he laid down rules like the ones we have described (about the ban on buying precious metals and the equal division of booty), even when there transpires from his choices what we have described as a "prophetic" vocation, they were always the dispositions of a commander in the field rather than those of a legislating sovereign. He was concerned to stop acquisitive greed and personal rivalries from taking the edge off his men's combat readiness, and to attract as many new recruits as he could, not to build an alternative model of society. For the moment, this must have been just a faint glow in the background, nothing more than a dimly perceived objective or prospect. For now, military considerations must have been paramount. Which meant, above all, movement, rapidity, compactness—as befitted a well-led army ready for battle.

Diodorus, again, tells us that the Sicilian rebels managed to field up to two hundred thousand men—a clear exaggeration. But certain important parts of the island, especially inland areas, were wrested for a long time from Roman control. The insurrection was still under way in 133. According to Appian, Tiberius Gracchus, tribune that year, was able to cite it as a topical example of the real risks caused by concentrating large numbers of slaves on *latifundia*, and as an argument in favor of the proposal to rebuild the pattern of small and medium-sized farm properties based on free labor, along the lines of the republican agrarian tradition. It was not until 132 that the consul Rupilius, finally sent from Rome at the head of a regular army, managed to retake the cities and crush the revolt. When all hope of survival had vanished, Diodorus recounts that Eunus, besieged in Henna by the Roman legions, roused his followers and urged them on to final resistance by staging "a production of mimes, in which the slaves acted out scenes of revolt from their individual masters, heaping abuse on their arrogance and the inordinate insolence that had led to their destruction"—an improvised theater of desperation, which gave fresh expression to the culture and inventiveness of those who had been deprived of their voice and history.

But Sicily—despite the repression and a significant attempt, conducted by Rupilius himself in 131, to reorganize the legal and administrative system—would remain a dangerous hotbed of insubordination, probably fed by maverick remnants of the vanquished rebel force (Eunus, oddly spared, died several years later in a Roman jail). In the meantime, lesser episodes took place in Nuceria and Capua, where a young Roman from an equestrian family, Titus Vetius, having fallen hopelessly in love with another man's slave girl and unable to buy her because of the exorbitant price requested by the owner, seized her, incited his own four hundred slaves to rebel, and at their head began to sack the nearby *villae*—an incomparable example, for Diodorus, of the dangerousness of the times: emotional excess and social disorder. When the praetor, Lucius Lucullus, sent from Rome, managed, with a subterfuge, to get the better of the rebels, Vetius had gathered together over 3,500 men.

Then, after years of unrest, a second widespread Sicilian revolt broke out in 104. The African war against Jugurtha had just finished, and the previous year the Roman legions had been heavily defeated by the Cimbri at Arausio, in Gaul. The insurrection began this time in the western part of the island. It was led by a man named Salvius, of unknown origins, but "who was reputed to be skilled in divination and was a flute-player of frenetic music at performances for women"—once again servile rebelliousness interwoven with popular credulity. No important cities were taken. Instead, the movement was concentrated in the countryside, where the rebels split up into three columns that moved with relative independence. Here too, the slaves' struggle was accompanied by the parallel one of the rural plebeians: "those without means, impelled alike by poverty and lawlessness, streamed out into the country in swarms, drove off the herds of cattle, [and] plundered the crops." In the area of Segesta and Lilybaeum, the rebels were led by a former Cilician slave, Athenio, who, after several run-ins and misunderstandings, joined forces with Salvius, and succeeded him after the latter's death. The resistance continued until 101, when the rebel chief was definitively beaten (and killed) by one of that year's consuls, Manius Aquilius—the other was Gaius Marius.

· 9 ·

According to Caecilius of Caleacte, cited by Athenaeus, the Sicilian insurrections resulted in an enormous loss of human life: a million deaths. The figure is exaggerated, even supposing that the author included in the calculation not only the Sicilian revolts, but all the rebellions that occurred almost simultaneously in the empire. But it gives an idea of the extent of the uprisings, and the size of the masses involved—and no less probably, of the harshness of the repression as well.

Posidonius, as we have seen, linked the rapid spread of the revolts to the inhuman living conditions of the slaves, in the *latifundia* as in the mines. He was writing more or less in the years of Spartacus. Having traveled widely, he had formed an opinion about what the Roman Mediterranean had become. In Spain, he had observed the ruthless organization of labor, which was unrelenting: the slave miners continually asked to be put out of their misery and actively sought death, deemed preferable to unbearable suffering. In the mines of Laurion, in Attica, the situation would not have been any better. To Lucretius, at almost the same time, the slave's life appeared little different. Such judgments were certainly not unanimous among the educated elites of the empire: to Strabo, the great geographer of the Augustan age, for instance, Posidonius's descriptions seemed inappropriate and irksome. It was not the common view, just the one that, for various reasons, was less prejudicially hostile toward the slave world, and so for us, evidently, closer to the truth.

The philosopher of Apameia knew quite well that there had always been slave revolts: he was certainly aware of the attention given by Thucydides to the rebellions that had taken place back in the times of the Peloponnesian war, in the fifth century, when more than twenty thousand slaves had fled from Attica during the Spartan occupation of Decelea; not to mention more ancient cases of insubordination in Rome, between the fifth and the third century, gathered by a tradition that would then be reported by Livy. But what Posidonius must have seen as a specific characteristic of his own age was the "worldwide" (in the ancient sense of the word) spread of chattel slavery in step with the establishment of an economy based on trade and the increasingly intense exploitation of nature—from *latifundia* and *villae* to mines. The ever more marked connection between slavery and the "worldwide" scale of the empire (we would say between slavery and the functioning of a sketchy "world economy," the first in history) entailed, for him, the inevitable human degradation of the slaves. This prompted them to rebel in different places and circumstances, with a simultaneity whose meaning was inescapable: "To most people," writes Diodorus, "these events came as an unexpected and sudden surprise, but to those who were capable of judging affairs realistically they did not seem to happen without reason."

Posidonius was by no means a radical critic of slavery (though some had existed, on the margins of Greek culture; Aristotle alludes to them in passing in his *Politics*), nor was he imagining a world without slaves. He just limited himself to making a distinction, as Theopompus, a fourth-century Greek historian, had done, between a good form of slavery "according to nature"—patriarchal and domestic, integrated into kinship ties and the powers of the head of the family— and a "degenerate" one, spawned by the development of trade and production for markets (formerly Athenian and now, on a much larger scale, Roman), which was based on the abuse of chattel slaves. Only the second led to disaster, to the fatal outbreak of a dual and specular violence: that fed by the arrogance and excessiveness of the masters, and that fueled by the hatred of the slaves.

Nor can Posidonius be considered a democrat, not even in the ancient meaning of the word. Instead, he was a traditionalist close to the Roman senatorial nobility (Pompey was for him the man of destiny). And he developed his polemic against "degenerate" slavery entirely in the context of a declared aversion for the Roman-Italic equestrian groups, toward those social ranks of merchants, speculators, and business-mongers whose craving for profits had upset an institution "according to nature," which had originally fitted in well with a design of universal harmony, and transformed it into a mechanism of brutalization and abuse that would incur divine punishment.

Posidonius's suggestion was however quite inapplicable to the reality of the Roman empire. The idea of a return to a patriarchal style of peasant society, like the one yearned for in the poetry of Hesiod—basically autarchic, with strictly respected hierarchies of kinship relations, far removed from the ruinous effects of wealth and money—was an illusion.

Yet these were not just the dreams of a nostalgic philosopher idealizing a bygone age. Tiberius Gracchus, as we have seen, had been equally suspicious of the large concentrations of chattel slaves, and had been unsympathetic to the needs of *latifundia* owners. And he had been no less worried by the Sicilian insurrection. His fears undoubtedly had other origins, and other motivations. He was not a thinker, and he was a democrat (despite coming from a family of nobles), at least according to the Roman conception of politics. But the solution he had envisaged, though better developed and more realistic than Posidonius's utopia—it was, after all, a legislative program—anticipated an essential aspect of it. Tiberius also proposed to put a brake on the concentration of slaves with a return to the past through the restoration, by law, of the model of small-scale peasant landownership that, by favoring the rural plebeians, would enable the reestablishment of a farmer-citizen-soldier society—the same one that had made the republic great, and which the formation of the empire had almost completely destroyed.

Both perspectives basically shared a common archaizing trait. For the troubled philosopher, friend to the nobility, just as for the politician favorably disposed to the agrarian plebs, the degeneration of slavery could only be fought by looking backward, by searching in the past for models of social life that could do without the form of production that had so radically altered their own times.

They were impossible solutions: the apparently realistic one of the politician no less than the patent utopia of the thinker, as history was hastening to demonstrate. But inscribed within their common implausibility, hidden and seemingly reversed, lay an element essential for understanding what was happening—the novelty of the Roman present and its contradiction, the existence of a very close tie between slavery and imperial "modernization," which even the most severe critics were unable to disentangle by looking ahead, but only by imagining a leap backward, a full-blown restoration of a now remote and lost age.

And Spartacus? He would definitely have had some information about the great Sicilian revolts—a servile memory of such events must have been alive in Capua, at least from the episode of Vetius onward; and he probably knew about the Gracchi as well. On the other hand it is possible he had never heard of Posidonius and his theories. But his measures against the purchase of precious metals and for the equal division of plunder— though dictated by the need for discipline in the field— seem to have been inspired by the same antimercantile ideals, with an egalitarian tendency that also appears to have been directed more toward the restoration of a distant patriarchal and communitarian past than the future of an already urbanized and complex society.

Certainly, in the winter of 73–72, during the long nights in the mountains and woods of Lucania, he would mainly have considered a military and political way out, thinking about how to continue his campaign. But it would have been precisely from a strategic appraisal of the situation that he formed the idea which was to emerge the following spring, with the realization that in order to retain hope, he had to extend his objectives, and to combine, more than he had done until then, arms and politics, military victories and insurrectional success.

The consuls in 72 were Lucius Gellius Publicola and Gnaeus Cornelius Lentulus Clodianus. At the request of the senate, "shaken . . . by the disgrace . . . of being kept at bay by a band of rebels," and seriously concerned by the turn of events, they decided to take over direct command of the operations. Neither had any significant experience in war. The former, who was over sixty, had studied rhetoric and cultivated some philosophic pursuits; the latter was a fair orator. The aristocratic education of the age still tended to unify fields rather than encouraging specialist skills and knowledge, and tried to hold together civil virtues and military responsibilities.

They were not easy years for the imperial republic, forced as it was to wage war on two fronts: in Spain, where the ambitious Pompey, who had trained under Sulla, was engaged, with a special proconsular command, in retaking control of the country, which had passed almost entirely into the hands of the rebel Sertorius (who had served under Marius and had been a praetor in 83); and in the East, where Lucius Licinius Lucullus (consul in 74) was trying to counter the renewed attacks of Mithridates, who had occupied Bithynia, only recently annexed to the empire. We can estimate that Rome had no less than one hundred and ten thousand frontline troops occupied overall in the two theaters—twenty-one or twenty-two legions—to which we must add the forces stationed in Gaul and Macedonia (about another eight legions). Not much was left for Italy.

The consuls began the campaign with four legions (correcting an oversight by Appian), probably recruited in great haste after the defeat of Varinius. Inexperienced soldiers—again—led by commanders who were not much better. They immediately marched south to reestablish contact with the enemy.

Spartacus decided not to wait for them in Lucania. Abandoning their winter camps, he and his men also began to move, heading north along the Apennine Ridge. We cannot say exactly when they started out, though presumably no later than March, given the following events. How big was his force? Almost certainly no more than forty thousand combatants (the figure mentioned by Orosius, much more credible than Appian's seventy thousand)—with a following of unknown size made up of women, children, and men unable to bear arms. They were well trained, in the Roman manner, as Caesar, who understood such matters, would observe impartially. The winter had not been wasted. They may also have adopted the Roman organization of units: legions, cohorts, centuries. In general, they must have been well equipped. They had had the time and opportunity to produce new weapons. In some cases they made do with unorthodox equipment—wickerwork shields, for instance, covered with animal skins.

But at this point, just after setting off, they decided to split up into two columns: one, thirty thousand strong, led by Spartacus, and the other, under Crixus, of ten thousand—higher figures, though present in the tradition, do not seem to me to be reliable.

Why did they separate? Plutarch and Appian say nothing. The temptation is to see it as the outcome of a conclusive divergence of views, following earlier disagreements. But Spartacus's subsequent behavior seems to belie such an interpretation, for which there is not a shred of evidence. It cannot be excluded that a certain hostility—personal maybe, but more probably between the different ethnic groups—to the idea of continuing their adventure together may have played a role. I believe however that it was basically the consequence of a broadly accepted strategic choice. Spartacus was aware of the Romans' difficulties in putting together an adequate force, with their best legions occupied from one end of the Mediterranean to the other. Italy looked wide open, almost undefended; the moment offered an unrepeatable opportunity. The best thing to do was to advance along distinct routes, in an attempt to multiply their ambushes and attacks. Striking simultaneously in various directions: going northward, but at the same time testing the Romans' capacity to respond on different fronts. Besides, smaller armies, operating in nonadjoining areas, had more scope for provisioning, an issue that must have played continually on Spartacus's mind.

But above all, I think another element weighed heavily on the decision: the heart of the major change that had taken shape in the winter, which reveals the first sign of Spartacus's new policy. At that time, memories of the Social War were still fresh in Italy: when less than twenty years earlier, in 90, many populations—

Osci, Sabellians, Marsi, Samnites—weary of unequal alliances, had risen up in arms against Rome, especially in the central and southern regions. The revolt then had been suffocated only with difficulty, following a general concession of Roman citizenship—a measure that stretched the constitutional borders of the republican "polis," which had originally taken in nothing more than the capital itself and the immediately surrounding rural area, to the whole of the Peninsula, from the Po Valley to the Strait of Messina. Spartacus wanted to reopen that wound to his own advantage. Moving in separate forces would bring them into contact with more territories and populations, creating greater opportunities for involvement and perhaps solidarity—a hope that, as things stood, was not entirely unfounded. Hannibal had tried to do the same, almost a 150 years earlier, long before the Social War—to win Italy over to his side against Rome. Military victories and political initiative. Why not try again? Admittedly, Hannibal had been at the head of a real army, and not a force arising out of a slave revolt. But this servile origin could fade into the background if new alliances were formed and the insurrection reached a more substantial critical mass.

The Roman army divided as well, to counter the enemy maneuver. While Lentulus tried not to lose Spartacus, Gellius headed, with two legions, toward Crixus, who in the meantime had arrived in Apulia. In the Roman ranks was a young Marcus Porcius Cato, later known as Uticensis, who was gaining his first experience of warfare. He was just over twenty.

What exactly happened is unknown. Crixus must have been a brave warrior, but not a capable commander. Away from Spartacus, and without his discipline and tactical inventiveness, at the first test he proved unable to cope. Maybe his men—for the most part Celts—split up straight away in search of easy prey and plunder: precisely what Spartacus—but he alone—had succeeded in avoiding (though we should not slip into ethnic prejudices). Gellius, whose high command included a "man of decision" (as Cicero defined him), Quintus Arrius, praetor the previous year, pressed on his heels, and then fell upon him near the Gargano Promontory stretching out into the Adriatic at the furthermost point of the Peninsula—an area of harsh terrain, covered at that time by forests, mostly of oaks. Crixus was caught unawares; much more was required—nothing less than the talent of Spartacus—to oppose the Roman war machine, even if not the cream of its fighting force. The Romans struck "unexpectedly" (so Plutarch says), and cut the rebel force to pieces, notwithstanding desperate resistance. Crixus himself fell in the battle, together with two-thirds of his men.

Spartacus was immediately informed—communications had never been interrupted between the two columns. The two consular armies—of Lentulus and of Gellius and Arrius—now converged with the intention to trap him in a pincer movement. After the rout of Crixus, a certain numerical parity had been reestablished: no fewer than four legions took part in the enveloping maneuver.

But Spartacus, who had continued his northward march, snatched the initiative from the Romans before the vise closed around him. He thrust into the gap between the two enemy armies moving up the Apennines from the south and east, and attacked them separately: first Lentulus, then Gellius, and defeated both.

Actually, a fragment of Sallust seems to suggest that the Roman legions might have met up, even if only when Lentulus's troops were already heavily engaged; but it is just a hypothesis. At any rate, they were not battles of annihilation, although the clash with Lentulus, in the Apennines between Tuscany and Emilia, was particularly bloody: the consul had taken a stand with some of his troops on high ground, which he held with a double line of defenses, suffering heavy casualties. In the end, both Roman commanders managed to pull back toward the south, despite losing supplies and equipment in the retreat.

But by now a third Roman army was converging on Spartacus: the garrison of Cisalpine Gaul, which the rebels had now reached in their northerly drive, commanded by the magistrate governing the province in that year, the same Gaius Cassius Longinus who had been consul in 73, aided by one of the praetors of 72, Gnaeus Manlius. Spartacus took them on straight away, near Mutina (Modena), and soon got the better of them.

This sequence of successes is astonishing. Unfortunately, it is impossible to reconstruct the course of the clashes: the loss of the *Histories* has erased everything. But we can readily imagine the crucial role Spartacus's presence must have played in the outcome of the battles. All it took was for him to be absent, and everything resumed its more natural course. With Crixus, the former slaves immediately went back to being what history had basically forced them to be: a hopeless rabble. Spartacus, in sharp contrast, had miraculously succeeded in transforming them into an army—in some respects into a "Roman" army, according to Caesar's pondered judgment—and had led them superbly. These victories against entire legions would be quite unexplainable without confident strategic leadership, tactical acumen, rapid execution, and perfect timing. And all this with no previous knowledge either of the terrain or the settlements configuring his theaters of operation, while the Romans were on their home patch. He improvised everything, computing information as he decided, just as Caesar, campaigning in Gaul not long afterward, would combine geographic discovery, anthropological observation, strategic design, and tactical assurance.

Spartacus was by now on the edge of the Po Valley, and for the second time after the autumn of the previous year he seemed to be the master of his destiny. To the north, the road to the Alps was wide open, either toward Transalpine Gaul or toward Illyria; to the south, only the battered forces of the two consuls lay between him and Rome. A year earlier he had still been a slave fighting in the arena, about to attempt a desperate escape. Now he had men, arms, space, and time—everything a field commander could possible wish for. With a few quick, skillfully executed moves he had once again turned fortune in his favor, after the debacle of Crixus. He was at the peak of his exploits, and every option was open to him. The season was holding fair and summer was on the way—the summer of 72, the second of his great adventure.

THREE

THE LOSER

· 1 ·

WHAT were Spartacus's plans? Nothing of what he had in mind is known to us directly. His psychology and mental landscape are completely inaccessible; a fascinating theme, but entirely obscure. Our protagonist's intentions can only be deduced from the bare sequence of his actions.

If he had thought, even if only now, of leaving Italy, he had a golden opportunity to do so. And if, previously, he had been held back by the attitude of Crixus and his followers, as part of the ancient tradition seems to suppose, now he was on his own. He had already pushed a long way north, to the edge of the Po Valley, and between him and the Alps, both east and west, the Roman military apparatus, following the defeat of Cassius Longinus and Manlius, was nothing more than a flimsy veil that could be torn apart anywhere and at any time.

But Spartacus, once again, did not choose this path—quite simply because he had never wanted to. He had always pursued other aims.

He organized a grandiose funeral for Crixus—further proof there had been no rift between them—in the course of which he sacrificed three hundred Roman prisoners (for Orosius it was four hundred), making them fight to the death in gladiatorial games in honor of the fallen chief: a symmetrical and sensational reversal of roles between victims and executioners, destined to make a powerful emotional impact on the spectators, and which gave Spartacus's army the tangible sensation of the position they had achieved, measured against the memory of their very recent past. They had become an army of free men, engaged in a tough campaign in enemy territory, and authorized by the customs of war to treat their prisoners as slaves.

Then, having destroyed their nonessential baggage, killed the surplus animals, and summarily executed the remainder of their Roman prisoners—these things happened in ancient wars—Spartacus switched his direction of march and aimed south, toward the capital. He "marched on Rome," writes Appian unequivocally. Florus says the same, while it would even appear from Ampelius that Spartacus had already decided to burn it. A realistic assessment of his forces suggests he had no less than sixty to seventy thousand fighting men.

At this point, again in Appian's account, a small detail crops up which, though seemingly negligible, may have been deliberately retained by the source who first reported it. We must consider the information with care.

As Spartacus was completing his final preparations before moving off, "many deserters offered themselves to him, but he would not accept them." There is no reason to doubt these few words, which Appian probably transcribed from Sallust (or perhaps from Livy). And so? What prompted this decision, if, just a few months earlier, between Campania and Lucania, Spartacus had been willing to recruit anyone capable of grasping a weapon?

I believe this slight incongruence—like a barely perceptible blemish in the weave of Appian's account—hides an important trace that explains the marked change which took place in the strategy of the war—the same one we imagined being conceived over the long months of the preceding winter, and already anticipated in the separation from Crixus. At the base of it we can find a new perception Spartacus had formed of himself and of his great venture.

The deserters were rejected now because Spartacus no longer regarded himself as being at the head of an army of fugitives and drifters, but behaved like a genuine commander in the field, a victorious warlord from the East placed by divine predestination at the head of a real army committed to achieving a goal that would alter the course of history: to strike at the heart of Roman power and snatch Italy from its dominion. In the same months, fighting was also under way in Thrace, against the proconsul Marcus Terentius Lucullus, who, as consul in 73, had, with Gellius, witnessed, without intervening, the start of the revolt and the defeat of the praetor Varinius. Further east war was raging with Mithridates. It is likely that the concomitance of events was known to the rebels in Italy, and this must have strengthened the feeling that they were the protagonists of a great design. We can imagine that Spartacus identified with this self-representation. What in the winter of 73–72 had perhaps been nothing more than a first intuition now took on, after the victories in spring, much greater substance.

In the new perspective, slavery was, if not forgotten, at least put to one side. It was no longer slaves, deserters, and irregulars—the "dregs of the people," according to the expression later used by Cicero—who had to be united. If the objective was Rome, the quality and clout of his allies had to change. He would need to be able to count on more widespread revolts (we will see which shortly, in a second revelatory detail), and to organize recruitment and the search for resources on a different basis. An attempt had already been made by sending Crixus to stir up Apulia and to rekindle the spirit of the anti-Roman uprisings at the time of Hannibal and the Social War. But the inexperience of the Gallic leader—who had possibly been overrated by Spartacus—had stymied the plan. Now was the moment to try again, and to build around the victorious army something resembling a real system of alliances, finally rooted in the territory. For this objective, deserters served no good purpose, and might even be counterproductive. Instead, a marked change was required in the way the war was being conducted.

My conjecture, in a word, is that the recent successes against the consular armies had given decisive impetus to Spartacus's ambitions and designs, projecting them outside the orbit of slavery. The man planning to head straight for Rome no longer saw himself as a former gladiator—and nor could such a goal be achieved by limiting the revolt to the slaves. The self-perception now cultivated by Spartacus was that of a great anti-Roman commander (who had also coincidentally spent some time as a prisoner of his enemies), who placed no limits on his strategy to carry out a memorable undertaking: to defeat, on their own territory, and by exploiting their weak points, the masters of the world.

Spartacus was taking new models as his inspiration. And in those circumstances, his point of reference could not have been anyone other than Hannibal—whose work he wanted to complete. He believed he could grasp the opportunities opened up by the new wounds of the Social War and possibly also by developments in Rome's internal political struggle. A comparison with the Carthaginian leader surfaces, in fact, in Eutropius and Orosius, probably suggested by Livy: and it is not hard to believe the motif dated back to the time of Spartacus—the new Hannibal.

· 2 ·

What we are proposing is the only plausible explanation for understanding the crucial months of the summer of 72. Two overlapping elements have long contributed to obscuring it: one ancient, the other modern. The first is the very solid image built up by the

Roman tradition, which sought, probably with the exception of Sallust (we will return to this) to nail Spartacus down to the role of the fugitive slave. He could not possibly be anything other than that. And so, following the stereotype of the escapee, his main aim could only be to return home, his goals limited in any case to the servile world, or better, to the way in which the Romans represented that world—to the slave anthropology of the masters. Everything else was inevitably cut from the literary and historic construction of the character, and appears only, and confusedly, on the outer edges of the figure. We, on the other hand, are trying to bring back into the center of the stage precisely this hidden side.

The second element that has obstructed our understanding relates instead to the modern legend of Spartacus as an interpreter and a leading example of a more or less latent "class consciousness" of the Roman slaves. In this picture of events, his revolt is represented as a somehow conscious attempt at a "slave revolution"— intended to overthrow the servile foundations of imperial society.

Both these points of view—the ancient and the modern—have ended up supporting each other, at least in one essential respect, which is precisely the one we are calling into question: the confinement of the Spartacus story and its significance within the horizons of Roman slavery—a boundary not to be exceeded in any interpretation.

But they are both prejudices, and equally unfounded.

We have already talked about the first one. Spartacus never intended, not even at the outset, to flee from Italy, but only to fight Rome in the most favorable conditions possible. And, from a certain moment onward, let's say from the beginning of the campaign of 72, and especially after his victories over the consular armies in the Apennines, this decision took the form of a plan to attack the city of Rome itself, a quite unrealistic proposition if the struggle remained nothing more than a slave uprising. Spartacus had something different in mind: an initiative capable of striking at Rome's overall hegemony in Italy, and (probably) the aristocratic control of the *res publica*. At least from the spring of 72, he had stopped regarding himself as a rebel slave chief, acting instead as the leader of an anti-Roman movement designed to rise far above the servile origins of the revolt.

As for the second element, we come now to the crux of a very serious misunderstanding, which deserves to be examined at greater length.

In reality, and looking far beyond the Spartacus story, no form of "class consciousness" ever existed in the history of Rome—least of all among the slaves— for the simple reason that in ancient history there is no detectable presence of real "classes," in the modern and powerful sense of the word; just social stratifications, at times very complex, whose dynamics and contrasts, however, never produced class structures as such. Their inception would have presupposed conditions which never arose in that context. The establishment, that is, of a relationship, on a large scale and with legally equal parties, between land and factory owners on the one hand, and peasants and workshop laborers on the other, as would happen in modern Europe between possessors of the means of production and (free) possessors of labor. Such a relationship never emerged in ancient societies, not even in first-century Rome, stymied as they were by the spread of slavery. Intrinsically coercive in nature, it prevented labor from coming onto the market in a widespread way as a commodity sellable by free workers, and consequently to give rise to a class structure. The latter always presupposes, in fact, the existence of a labor market, with the tensions that are historically released between the legal equality of the parties and the substantive inequality in their social and economic power.

In ancient societies, by contrast, the commodity was the whole slave, and not just his labor-power. The shackle of personal dependence—the servile condition that reduced people to things—erased the decisive separation between workers as persons and the sale of their labor—the essence of modernity—thus impeding the creation of that scission which, in the industrial world, is constitutive of class relations. The existence of this kind of subordination had, in ancient societies, an entirely noneconomic origin and regulatory order, which represented an insuperable obstacle to the formation of classes because it never set workers in front of land or factory owners, but always left a single player on the field: the figure who, according to the peculiar model of the overlord, was at the same time the owner of land (and more rarely of factories) and the master of slaves. Nor did it enable the development of the self-sustained production process typical of modern economies, because while the working condition of the free wage laborer is in a certain sense "created" by the factory and by the contract, the servile condition of the slave was not "created" by the *latifundium* or by the *villa*, but by noneconomic causes such as plundering or captivity in war. A slave could be bought and sold, but could not be "produced," as such, by the economic system. In Latin there was not even a word to express the (nonexistent) notion of abstract human labor, in its full modern sense. This would come into being in Europe not before the Industrial Revolution.

Roman-Italic society in the first century was certainly very complex in structure, and included all sorts of strands, from the "senatorial order" of the large agrarian holdings and the "equestrian order" of business groups—merchants, usurers, tax farmers, owners of factories and workshops—to the remaining landowning peasant farmers, the urban plebs, the slave masses, and the rural dispossessed. And it was also shot through with ferocious political conflicts (something will be said about these shortly). But it always remained a society of "orders," of "statuses," not of classes, where the economy played an important but not decisive role in the forming of social hierarchies. Other functions carried greater weight, in different circumstances and ages: kinship relations, politics and offices, military careers, bureaucratic power. A world at any rate incapable—for cultural reasons and for ones linked to the intrinsic fragility of a purely slave-based structure of production—of triggering a genuine mechanism of capitalistic accumulation, or something similar to an industrial takeoff, and never able to create "bourgeois" social strata whose main goals were productivity and reinvestment rather than property revenue. We are still in the presence of unilinear societies with a strong aristocratic imprint, at the base of which lay plebeian masses rendered shapeless by the absence of work and social ties; and, even further down, enormous numbers of slaves who, in the countryside, produced almost all the wealth. It is in fact hardly a coincidence that in all the imperial territories, from the Rhine to the Euphrates, no trace has ever been found, archaeologically or otherwise, of any settlement pointing to the existence of a single industrial area comparable to modern ones, even of the eighteenth century.

I believe therefore that the arbitrary spread of the paradigm of "classes" and their (eventual) forms of consciousness, to the point of becoming a kind of universal key for historic interpretation, has been (and still is today) one of the worst ways in which our knowledge of the past has been muddied by European culture since the nineteenth century. The division of societies into classes—if we do not give this word a merely generic and metaphoric meaning that runs roughshod over any social-analytic definition—is a phenomenon pertaining only to societies born around the time of the Industrial Revolution, and is thus limited to their history. The "class struggle," a grand and generative element of Western modernity (though, to be rigorous, not all of it, if we consider the social history of the United States), applies to a specific model of conflict and collective subjectivity, the scheme of which cannot be transposed out of its historic age, neither backward in time to explain Rome or Greece, nor forward, into our postindustrial present—as has been coming very clear to us in recent years.

The Roman slave revolts thus never took on "class" connotations, either in Sicily or elsewhere. The insurrections were sparked by servile masses ephemerally united by what they considered to be a common misadventure from which to liberate themselves, not by the shared perception of the need to overthrow the economic system once and for all. And in fact none of the behavior we are able to reconstruct authorizes us to suppose—if not as a modern projection—that Spartacus ever deliberately acted in the name of all the slaves of Rome, or fought for their general release, or at any rate felt bound by a classist scheme. Nor, even less, that in the servile masses of the first century there was an awareness of a common horizon, of a tie with some sort of "political" or "economic" value, and that they ever saw Spartacus as a universal liberator.

Admittedly, the thought of the Roman slaves is a lost universe: no voice has ever arrived from that world, if not filtered through their masters' sensibility and prejudices—writing was not for them. Similarly lost are virtually all the humble effects that filled their daily lives, because while innumerable possessions of the rich and powerful (large buildings, durable everyday objects) have come to light, it is much harder, despite the miracles of archaeology, to find poor people's things. Fashioned from lowly, perishable materials, they were immediately brushed away by time, erased—like feelings, folklore, states of mind—by the irreparable destructiveness history reserves for the memory of the weak.

We are however in a position to say that imperial slavery constituted a social galaxy shattered into a myriad of fragmented services and productive functions. Everything leads us to presume that highly diverse attitudes and personal choices took shape—from resistance and sabotage through to complete adherence to the style of life of the masters. Without a doubt, Spartacus had accepted into his ranks combatants largely or very largely of slave origin—he could not have done otherwise in the circumstances—and his presence alone represented a strongly destabilizing factor for the whole slave system, a danger of which the Romans were evidently well aware. But there is no evidence he was thinking of something resembling a "servile revolution." The possibility that his revolt might spread across the board, involving in a generalized way the masses of slaves living within the borders of the empire, was, in those years, more of a nightmare of the Roman-Italic landowners than a strategy of the Thracian commander: a specter generated by the terror of the masters rather than an option effectively pursued by their victims.

Once he had started heading south, the information about Spartacus's movements and the sequence of clashes becomes garbled in the sources available to us, and there are probably several points of confusion in Plutarch's account. But one thing is certain: Spartacus did not choose the most direct route to Rome. In that case he would not have moved far away from the Apennine Ridge and the big consular roads. Instead, he made a detour toward the east—as Hannibal had done after the Battle of Lake Trasimene in 217—and in the summer he was still in Picenum.

Why there precisely? The only plausible response is that he wanted, before attacking the capital, to bring significant parts of the population over onto his side, to acquire strategic depth, to gain a supportive territorial base for his army. Picenum had been one of the main hotbeds of revolt during the Social War, and now Spartacus was evidently trying to open up that sore again and to rebuild an anti-Roman front.

The consuls, who in the meantime had regrouped their legions and bolstered them with new recruits, moved to face Spartacus on "the borders" of the region. He did not try to elude them—now feeling quite confident of his strength—and the ensuing clash had the hallmarks of being a pitched battle, probably fought in two phases. It is likely that the Romans, in numerical inferiority, tried to envelop the enemy, attempting a broad flanking maneuver. But Spartacus did not fall into the trap, and managed to wipe out a Roman column—two legions strong, and commanded by a legate of the consuls, Mummius—that was trying to attack him from the rear ("many of his [Mummius's] men were slain, and many of them threw away their arms and fled for their lives"). Then he turned on the rest of the Roman forces, and repulsed them, inflicting heavy casualties. Rome was now very close indeed, and "the City was hardly less afraid that it had been when it had trembled with Hannibal thundering in arms before its gates." As before, the danger came from the east: the first time had been from the banks of the River Aufidius, after Cannae; now it was from the furthest border of Picenum. The Thracian commander was retracing the movements of the Carthaginian general.

Then something unexpected occurred. Spartacus, like his predecessor 150 years earlier, suddenly decided not to attack the city, and changed his plans. Why? Had he been overcome by a kind of "Hannibal syndrome" at the idea of finding himself before the walls of Rome?

We cannot exclude the possibility, especially as the imperial Rome of his time must have been much more forbidding than it had been at the end of the third century, and, after all, Spartacus did not have the backing (however distant) of the Carthaginian power. But, to really understand what happened, I believe we must look in another direction.

Let's follow Appian's account once again: "Spartacus changed his intention of marching on Rome. He did not consider himself ready as yet for that kind of a fight, as his whole force was not suitably armed, for no city had joined him, but only slaves, deserters, and riff-raff."

The first part of the explanation does not hold up: of course, Spartacus would not have had any significant siege machinery, nor, perhaps, the technology to build it. But by now his troops would certainly have been well armed, if he had fought—and won—at least two pitched battles against the consular armies between the spring and summer of 72, and we can readily imagine that other weapons had fallen into his hands following the favorable outcome of those clashes. And in any case, these shortcomings, if they ever existed, must already have been apparent to him before he started his march south, after Mutina—and yet they had not deterred him from aiming for Rome. Something else must therefore have changed his mind, after he had begun his approach, between the Po Valley and Picenum. And it is Appian himself who reveals it (this is the second detail mentioned above), albeit almost in passing: "no city had joined him."

Here, finally, is the reason! Appian (or his source) discloses the existence of the plan through the announcement—charged with consequences—of its failure. We have already seen how Spartacus rejected deserters arriving in his camps, judging it to be a propitious moment to find much more solid allies, and to raise his action onto a completely different plane. Now we know exactly what he was seeking: to bring entire cities onto his side. First-century Italy was already broadly urbanized. He could not hope to win by sticking exclusively to rural areas—the heart of Roman power lay in the cities. Spartacus wanted to transform his revolt into an Italic war and into a civil war.

He was not succeeding, though. Perhaps he had based his reckonings on information and promises that then proved unreliable—and now he gave up the attempt, abruptly faced by the turn of events. He had hoped his march on Rome would have been accompanied by a progressive enlarging of the anti-Roman insurrection, and so had deviated toward Picenum, in order to move into territory that seemed favorable for his design. At this point his plan had gone awry. Yet just the allusion to it by Appian, even if simply to record its nonrealization, reveals, much more than a thousand pieces of lost information, what the revolt had become in those months; the ripples it had created, the chances of it spreading, and probably even the efforts made in this direction; and how much—in social and political terms—must have hinged on it. Whole cities might even have joined the rebels!

But nothing appreciable had then come of it. And now Spartacus found himself without the allies he needed—and quite unequipped to achieve his great venture.

Exactly how he conducted his efforts to enlarge the political and social base of the insurrection, above all in the spring and summer of 72, is completely unknown to us. Nor do we have any idea if Sallust spoke about them openly. Certainly, it must have been, for the Romans, the most disturbing aspect of the entire episode: the one least in tune with the stereotype of the fugitive slave. We can readily imagine that they preferred to overlook it, and why just one phrase in Appian reveals its existence. But it is also reasonable to think that, in the absence of such implications, Sallust himself would not have devoted so much space and attention to the revolt and its protagonist in the *Histories*.

In any case, the rapidity of Spartacus's change of heart poses a question. How far must we judge his design to have been unrealistic? Was it just the fruit of exaggerated overconfidence, due to unhoped-for successes, without any real possibility of coming to be? In other words, should the idea of transforming a slave revolt into a general insurrection—an Italic war and a civil war—against the power of Rome be considered, bearing in mind the historic situation at the time, its core elements as well as its contingencies, nothing more than an impossible dream?

· 4 ·

The Spartacus meteor was setting the skies of Rome ablaze, in what was a crucial time for the republic and for the destiny of the empire. The century running from the Gracchi to Augustus was the most tumultuous and fascinating period of Roman history, and probably of the whole ancient world. An exceptional density of events shaped the character of the epoch: an age of instability and transition, but also of cultural and social innovations, of economic growth (drugged by war plunder), of new possibilities and perspectives, some pregnant with the future. It appears to us as a feverish and unparalleled laboratory, in which there would be outlined for the first time features not found again until much later in the path of European history, no sooner than the end of the Middle Ages—like the phantom of a modernity nebulously glimpsed and immediately lost from sight.

After the stormy decades from the Gracchi to Sulla, the state of suffering of the old republican institutions had reached its peak, in the same period in which an impetuous expansive thrust, desired by the aristocracy no less than by the big profiteers, was unifying the Mediterranean, and new masses of slaves were flowing into the Peninsula by the day, deeply modifying traditions and habits.

The difficulty was institutional and political, and in some respects social, rather than strictly economic. Never before had Italy seen such wealth, albeit distributed in a fathomlessly unequal way, and oriented much more toward accumulation and consumption by the privileged minorities than toward efficient forms of productive reinvestment. The performance of the slave-based economy was supporting a network of markets that had never been so developed and was reaching levels that would long remain unparalleled in the history of the West.

The political crisis manifested itself above all in terms of the dramatic crumbling of the forces that had guided, during the third and second century, the imperial rise of the republic. It had been a system built on the civic primacy of the small landowners, who were at the same time citizens, peasant farmers, and soldiers. This had produced a compact social bloc, reflected in a

parsimonious and austere nobility—not so very different, in their habits and lifestyles, from the people they
guided. But "worldwide" growth had swept away everything: it had ruined the small landowners, due to
the competition of the large slave estates; separated
from the people an increasingly affluent aristocracy;
and nurtured a group of profiteers and speculators, avid
and enterprising but with no genuinely "bourgeois"
vocation (the conditions did not exist for anything of
this sort), just eager to worm their way into noble
circles and perhaps even to supersede the old aristocratic families. The economic miracle resulting
from expansion—the cycle of war-plunder-tenders-
wealth-new wars—had yielded a formidable accumulation of resources: land, from one end of the Mediterranean to the other; slave labor; trade networks;
monetary liquidity. And it was thrusting onto the
scene for the first time—thanks also to mechanisms of
social mobility permitted by the new forms of military
recruitment—the forces, ambitions, expectations, and
needs of groups, above all from the cities of Romanized Italy, who were demanding access, recognition,
well-being, power. Beneath them, suffocating and
barely surviving, was a plethoric plebeian world what
had once been the Roman *populus* of landowning peasants. They were still free citizens, but no longer had
anything, having been made destitute by long spells of
military service and by the new slave economy, which
encouraged the conglomeration of estates and, by of-
fering labor at a very advantageous cost, permanently
gave them no access to work. Finally, at the bottom of

the heap, were the masses of slaves—whose appearance on the scene had literally shattered the popular base of the republic—almost invariably crushed by disciplinary practices exercised without restraint or experience by masters in search only of immediate profits.

The nobility had been unable to keep apace of such changes. Its crisis had deep-rooted causes, relating in part to the short-sightedness of its most prominent members (excluding Sulla, who died in 78, and, to some extent, Pompey, born in 106—he was almost the same age as Spartacus—who had been fighting in Spain against Sertorius since 77), but above all to the consequences of expansion and conquest, and the professionalization of the army after Marius.

Then there was the virtual collapse of the republican form of government, by now hopelessly outsized. The political institutions—like all the ancient entities of this type—could only function in the confines and for the restricted numbers of a city, a *polis:* they had no notion of representation through delegation, and presupposed the possibility of bringing together all the citizens in a single square and in just one day. But after the Social War, when the republic extended from the Strait of Messina to the Po Valley, the political and institutional setup became abnormally large, and inevitably moved toward implosion.

The senatorial aristocracy thus became imprisoned by an ungovernable system, besides being overwhelmed by its own opulence and by the task of managing a suddenly worldwide power. It was incapable of conceiving its role in terms of a new Italic municipal order, and even found it hard to integrate the new city elites emerging around the Peninsula. Its conditioned reflex remained, as usual, an oligarchic closing of ranks in defense of now unsustainable privileges.

To counter it there was nothing resembling a genuine democratic movement, not even in the ancient meaning of the term. Moreover, the political infighting contributed to the weakening of institutions (magistracies, senate, assemblies). Governmental practices based on tradition (no written constitution existed) were continually breached, and naked violence was recurrent, not to mention corruption and vote rigging. Everything took place within a restricted oligarchy, which included the leaders of both the Optimates and the Populares, and the military high command was exploited to involve the army increasingly in the contest for power—with the urban plebs used as a mass to be maneuvered by the opposing forces. The history of the clashes between factions—parties did not exist in the modern sense of the word—conveys an image of a ferocious struggle between loose-knit groups with no real ideas or any genuine and contrasting programs: a bitter conflict in which it is impossible to see the broad sweep of big themes or of marked alternatives. And the few times a precise social content did take shape, it always related exclusively to patrimonial issues: struggles for the cancellation of debts, or, in some instances, for the distribution of land, but never for labor, or for the system of production. Those were matters for slaves—about which nothing would be said for a long time yet.

Even the notion of a municipal Italic movement failed to emerge as a definite project, remaining nothing more than an intuition fleetingly outlined on the margins of that world. The harshness of the conflict always ended up closing in on itself; there was never any prospect of real change, of genuine innovation in the exercising of power or in the composition of the ruling groups. The whole of republican politics floundered in the threatening but inconclusive demagogy of the Populares faction and in the blind obstinacy of the nobility.

· 5 ·

An investigation into the origins of this deadlock would take us a long way back. We are in the presence of a remote and enduring trait in the history of Rome, traceable in part to the persistent existence of the oligarchic form—unlike Athens, or, with much clearer connotations of a precocious class system, medieval Florence, where the protracted and radical political opposition between nobles and demos (between *magnati* and *popolani* in Tuscany) produced a contrast much closer to the sensibility of the moderns. The shadow of this original antidemocratic twist is perfectly perceptible in Sallust, and translates in his writing into a kind of negative anthropology of political life, fueled by a gloomy moralism: "Few men desire freedom, most seek nothing more than just masters," reads a discouraging observation in the *Histories.*

The stalemate of politics, its blinkered and cruelly inconclusive vision, combined with a confused awareness of having reached a limit never previously touched, of dealing with dimensions and sizes that had multiplied in the space of a few decades, contributed to a widespread perception of being in a precarious and brittle limbo. A suddenly boundless empire, a military apparatus stretching over three continents, enormous numbers of slaves concentrated in relatively limited areas, vast wealth accumulated and displayed with great ostentation, the incredible growth of the urban plebs, above all in Rome, which attracted the destitute in search of refuge from all over Italy, posed risks and problems of control no one had had to cope with before. From the upper reaches of power to the lowest social strata, people lived with the constant expectation that the unthinkable might happen—the terrifying *res novae* about which Sallust writes so effectively: the terrible "novelties" feared by "all good land-owning citizens," as Cicero writes, yet secretly and darkly desired by a part of what had now become a shapeless plebeian mass. The idea of the new was associated exclusively with subversion and catastrophe—a surprising assimilation for us but perfectly understandable in a culture that had not elaborated, and did not possess, any idea of change for the better, of discontinuity, of the future as progress, but had to sterilize any transformation—however profound—in the frame, even if fictitious, of the already-seen, of the already-known, of the already-happened. Nothing was to be "for the first time."

Hanging over that world, then, was a blanket of disquiet and uncertainty, the sensation that with the crumbling of ancient traditions, and in the face of the new and vertiginous imperial situation, anything was now possible.

It was against this backdrop that Spartacus's venture was unfolding.

And it is certainly no accident that when, almost two centuries later, Tacitus also spoke in passing of the Thracian's deeds, he did so—drawn by a kind of irresistible magnetism—exclusively in relation to those "new things" by which "the people is at once allured and terrified": a connection undoubtedly inspired by Sallust (though we cannot say whether or not it was explicitly formulated in the *Histories*).

Now I believe that this link, which placed Spartacus not on the edge, but at the heart of the most serious crisis Rome had ever faced, and at the center of the fears it had raised, was not a retrospective invention of the ancient historians. I think it actually did exist, in the facts and the intentions, and that Spartacus really did try to step into the political and social vacuum which he somehow felt lay before him, and to take a leap into the dark. And that, at least in this sense, his plan had some substance, a significant grounding in the reality of the time.

Almost certainly Spartacus did not have a completely defined political and social program—after all, who did in that age? But if he attempted to bring peoples and cities over onto his side—and of this we are certain—he must have been capable of conveying a message, an invitation to mobilize in the name of understandable objectives that could be identified with and shared by its recipients. The two elements went hand in hand: if there was a strategy—and there was, without a doubt—there must also have been a proposal. And at this point we can advance a conjecture as to its content, grouping them around two important themes that defined Spartacus's culture as we are trying to uncover it.

The first, more specifically political one, must have relied on the existence, in Italy, of a latent anti-Roman secessionism lingering on despite the end of the Social War, and ready to explode at the first opportunity. On the gamble that it was possible to repeat, on the Peninsula, what Sertorius—another military organizer and talent of the first order—had not long since done in Spain. That is to say, to build, with the support of the local populations, an alternative power to that of Rome: something similar to an Italic alliance with a revanchist component, capable of grasping the occasion offered by what was a difficult moment for the empire—the war with Mithridates, the Iberian revolt—in order to establish himself and, perhaps, to forge contacts and agreements. Spartacus came from the East, which is precisely where, in those same years, Mithridates was fighting a battle to the last man against the empire.

The other aspect of Spartacus's message must have tried to play on the social conditions of the Italic plebs, and should be tied in with his prophetic and egalitarian vocation. A more proportionate redistribution of land had already been a "democratic" objective since the Gracchi: we can reasonably assume that Spartacus sent out some radical signals in this sense.

He certainly did not want to abolish slavery: nothing authorizes us to think so. Roman prisoners were treated by him as slaves, and as slaves were made to fight and die. The idea of a society without servile labor formed no part of the ancient Mediterranean cultures. The great revolts of the second and first centuries did not set themselves this aim. They just sought to overthrow local setups, and to exact vengeance on inhuman masters, not to uproot an overall system. Neither philosophical thought, nor political or legal experience, offered any points of reference. And, what's more, in all the criticisms raised about the uncontrolled spread of chattel slavery and the harsh conditions it entailed, the suggested alternative—as we have seen—looked to the past rather than to the future. It envisaged the restoration of a world of domestic autarchies, with a softer form of slavery, numerically limited and "according to nature," incorporated within the family structures of former times. Such visions were fed solely by literary commonplaces regarding a return to the virtuous poverty of the ancestors; models unable to do anything other than create a yearning for archaizing restorations, in which the rejection of the excesses of slavery inevitably carried with it a repulsion toward large-scale trade, money, and mercantile networks. Basically, toward everything that was now an inerasable feature of Roman civilization, guaranteeing economic performances that underpinned the whole social structure of the empire: urban life, mass consumption, military and administrative bodies, intellectual creativity.

Nothing leads us to believe that Spartacus went beyond these views. After all, even in the slave revolts in the New World colonies, in the seventeenth and eighteenth centuries, analogous shades of archaizing restoration would be repeated, as if, from a viewpoint within a slave society, it was not really possible to see any other alternative.

The two levels on which Spartacus tried to move— the anti-Roman feeling of the Italic communities and the unrest among the plebs in the cities and country-side of the Peninsula, Rome included—were not to-tally imaginary: they lay within the horizons of the age. The slave world remained, relatively speaking, on the edges of this design. It had been the point of de-parture, and continued to be a reserve on which to draw to fuel the revolt—but nothing more.

Spartacus tried to wedge his insurrectional strategy into what might effectively have proved to be a fault line in the system of Roman dominion: along the join between the simmering plebeian masses (the old *populus* of the republic), the disquiet of the Italic communi-ties, and the institutional and political withering away of aristocratic rule—with the cracks of the slave system in the background.

It is hard to regard the plan as entirely unrealistic: the points of rupture were the same as those generat-ing the nightmare (and expectation) of the *res novae*— the uncertainty, pregnant with fear, that was envelop-ing the republic.

Ten years after the flight of Spartacus, another protagonist would attempt to play on almost the same elements: Lucius Sergius Catilina. But in this case, the social provenance was spectacularly reversed: Catiline was a noble, who in the sixties had been a praetor and a candidate for the consulate. He came from the heart of Roman power, and not from a gladiator camp; he had fought with Sulla, and maintained contacts (we do not know how close) with the young Caesar. His subversive design did not start with the slaves, but ended up reaching them as well, or at least came close to doing so. Whatever the perspective, the mental and social circuit was the same: "he [Catiline] proposed to encourage an insurrection of slaves in the city." And he met with the same lack of success, all the more so because in this case, as Gaius Gracchus and Lucius Cornelius Cinna had previously found, the slave masses, suddenly embroiled by desperate masters in affairs over which they had no control, did not respond.

Catiline appealed to young bankrupt aristocrats, penniless veterans of Sulla, and presented himself as an agitator of the Roman plebs, promising the cancellation of debts and the proscription of the rich. He sought alliances in Picenum, in Apulia (the same places touched on by Spartacus), and in Etruria.

If the *Histories* had survived, the symmetry likening Spartacus and Catiline in Sallust's interpretation would emerge much more sharply. But even with what little can be read, the parallels between the long account of the Thracian's revolt in the third and fourth books of the *Histories* and the monograph *(Catilinae coniuratio)* about the conspiracy of the subversive aristocrat are evident. For Sallust both epitomized the decadence of the republic, observed in a specular fashion from its highest and lowest points: in the plans of a fugitive slave and in the behavior of a noble who had arrived at the threshold of the consulate. Exceptional men with uncommon courage, both (for Sallust) embodied the much-feared *res novae,* the disorientation and worries of the age, and were protagonists of an attempt to overthrow the constituted order by trying to stir up the murkiest and most troubled depths of Roman-Italic society. In the first case, by gathering together an army of fugitive slaves; in the second, a cluster of young maverick aristocrats—two episodes that could have had very serious consequences, and that, in a well-governed society, would have been unthinkable.

But the point—and Sallust clearly could not have realized this—was that the success of a subversive solution fed by the lowest social orders, even if its leader came from outside such spheres (as in the case of Catiline), would have presupposed the existence of ties, alliances, and cultures that only a class structure could have provided, and which, instead, was totally missing in that world. And it was precisely this limit that proved the undoing of Spartacus, and later, of Catiline— the inability to trigger something resembling an authentic revolution.

Spartacus's plan was therefore both realistic and overambitious. Realistic, because it played on what were effectively the weak points of the power he was up against: the difficult political and social relations with the Italic communities, the presence of potentially uncontrollable plebeian masses, the slipshod and brutal administration of an all-pervasive slave system. And he also calculated, trying to exploit it to the full, the republic's occasional military weakness in the Peninsula, due to other wars elsewhere in the empire.

At the same time the idea was also overambitious, partly because, in his scheme to win the support of whole populations and cities, Spartacus underestimated the limit represented by the servile origins of his movement. When it came to the crunch, the strong prejudice against slaves ended up closing many doors and debarred many alliances that must have seemed possible to him. Above all, though, it was unrealistic because of the lack of a real political and social perspective to offer to the rebels, capable of going beyond a simple break with Rome and not merely looking to the past, to the autarchic egalitarianism of bygone days, idealized from the Gracchi to Posidonius; something with the power to hold together the urban and rural plebs and masses of slaves, not just with the closeness brought by desperation but by indicating the possibility of a new beginning.

We know quite well today that any idea of emancipation would necessarily have had to concern labor and the acknowledgment of its value as an essential element in the production of wealth: its twofold liberation from the bond of slavery and from the dissipation of the plebs. But this was something that could not be seen then, concealed as it was by the hapless condition of the slaves, or at any rate unable to take on a definite shape. It hung in the air, dreamt about more than actually glimpsed, only sensed as the fear of a subversive union capable of sparking a total overturning of the "natural" order of things—that is, of a revolution. But in Latin even the political significance of the word was unknown; for this we have to wait for the Founding Fathers.

Viewed from a certain angle, it might even seem that in those years the decisive passage was just one step away—that it would take virtually nothing for everything to become clear, at least in the thoughts of a rebel like Spartacus. And yet, for the most part, this is just an illusion springing from our condition as moderns, which invariably prompts us to look at ancient times in a retrospective way, and to measure past events against the yardstick of what would happen centuries later. In reality, a distance did exist, and it was not small, even if that epoch remains the only one, in the whole of Roman history, in which, amidst a tangle of contradictions, there seemed to appear, albeit for a brief flash, the incomplete image of a modernity destined to remain undefined until very much later.

· 7 ·

The Roman senate, in the meanwhile, had decided, not before time, to take adequate countermeasures. By now it was the beginning of autumn. The consuls were called back from the front and relieved of their commands. Responsibility for conducting the war was placed—probably with a special proconsulate looked upon favorably by the Populares as well—in the hands of Marcus Licinius Crassus, a man of great ambition and no less wealth, the future triumvir (together with Pompey and Caesar); heir of a prestigious Roman aristocratic family; the owner of land, mines, and an enormous number of slaves (probably thousands), who had added to his patrimony with unscrupulous building speculation. He seems to have taken advantage of the frequent fires that plagued Rome to snap up gutted houses cheaply, reselling them at an exorbitant price after they had been restored by the skilled slave laborers he had in abundant supply. Nonetheless, he was austere in behavior, inclined toward sobriety if not actually to avarice, not unversed in rhetoric and philosophy, and with some military experience. He had fought with Sulla at the Battle of the Colline Gate, commanding the right flank, and had brilliantly won the day. The previous year he had (perhaps) held the post of praetor, and was now looking for an occasion to emulate Pompey, whose fame and glory he wished to equal.

First of all, Crassus tried to reorganize and reinforce his army, while not losing contact with the enemy. A massive recruitment drive involving "all of those who, though advanced in years, still possessed enthusiasm for war" resulted in the formation of six new legions, which were added to the four consular ones already in the field. Rome now had about forty-five legions deployed on the chessboard of the empire— an impressive effort, unrivaled in those decades. Numerical parity with Spartacus's forces in Italy had now been largely reestablished. What's more, the senate asked (whether or not with the full agreement of Crassus is unknown) both Pompey, who was still in Spain, and Marcus Terentius Varro Lucullus, fighting, as we have already mentioned, in Macedonia against some Thracian populations, to return to Italy as quickly as possible. Together, the two commanders had little less than twenty legions. At this point, after the risky underestimations of the previous months, Rome wanted to employ crushing force.

That was not all. Crassus decided to inflict an exemplary punishment on the units that had performed worst in the previous clashes. Fifty men, extracted by lot from the five hundred deemed most guilty, were bludgeoned to death by their companions, in keeping with a terrible ancient custom revived for the occasion (a different version, which talks of up to four thousand dead, is not at all credible).

From Picenum, meanwhile, Spartacus was moving further and further south, where he evidently felt safer. Throughout his campaign he had displayed exceptional mobility—a talent he must have learnt in Thrace—and was using it to great effect, never giving the Romans a definite target. We are not able to piece together his route, and the whole picture of military operations during the autumn is fairly unclear. It is as if the Roman tradition brought down a veil over the events of these months, concentrating only on their conclusion. What is certain is that Spartacus went back to the Ionian Sea, where he reoccupied Thurii and the nearby mountains, and tried to resupply his forces with pack animals. He clashed on various occasions with

Crassus's forces, which were following him, in nondecisive battles. In one of these, it can be supposed in Lucania, the Roman legions managed to cut off from the bulk of the rebel army a column of ten thousand men, which was camped separately, perhaps because the order of march adopted by Spartacus was for large units to move at some distance from each other, or because the column was the rearguard of the whole army, which had stayed too far behind, with excessive confidence, to observe the Roman movements. In the ensuing battle, Crassus got the better of the rebel column, and wiped it out. According to Appian, two-thirds fell in battle; for Orosius (if he was referring, as is probable, to the same episode), six thousand were killed and nine hundred made prisoner. It was the Romans' first victory after the one over Crixus, and undoubtedly helped to improve morale and instill faith in their commander.

For Spartacus it was another sign that the tide of events was changing. His army was isolated. He was moving in sparsely populated territory, in the solitude of the mountains and forests of the south. And if supplies might not have been a problem in an area now familiar to him, and which was probably not entirely hostile—where it was still possible to find wine, wheat, oil, and pigs in a certain abundance—there had been no significant shifting of forces onto his side. After the trauma of the Social War, the Roman-Italic system seemed to be holding up, much more, perhaps, than Spartacus had expected. In the towns, not even the slaves followed him: no information exists, for that period, of any servile revolt in the main urban centers. At the time when the rebels seemed about to launch an attack on Rome, tens and perhaps hundreds of thousands of slaves were living there. And the urban plebs were no less numerous. Nothing suggests they lifted a finger. City life favored the development of capillary forms of subordination and integration, much more than the open spaces of the countryside. News would certainly have got around, but that was not enough. It is yet more evidence of the cultural and social fragmentation of those masses, and of their intrinsic passivity. The lack of class structures and the ingrained nature of the antislave prejudice prevented the revolt from developing either horizontally, involving the city slaves, or vertically, extending to the urban plebs. At the crucial moment, it dramatically revealed its agropastoral nature, its confinement to the slaves of the *latifundia* and the *villae*, and to the rural plebs, especially in the southern regions.

Following his initial success, Crassus continued to press Spartacus, trying to close him in a vise toward the south of Bruttium. He was in no hurry for a conclusive head-on battle; he preferred instead to wear down the enemy, to gradually reduce the scope for maneuvering in large spaces in which the Thracian commander had proved insuperable.

But Spartacus's military and political imagination was not yet exhausted. Once again he tried to exploit the opportunities offered by the territory he was in—the far south of Italy, between Lucania and Bruttium.

Why not try to cross over into Sicily, and from there continue the war in more favorable conditions?

It was a bold and perhaps rash plan, but far from senseless. Above all, it was not a desperate escape, as Appian and Florus seem keen to suggest (but not Plutarch, nor, from what we know, Sallust). Instead Spartacus devised, albeit in a great hurry, a full-scale operative plan to take control of the island (according to Plutarch), and not just to find refuge there. It is further proof, if any were still required, that Spartacus's enduring concern was to extend the social and political base of the revolt, to finally succeed in getting cities and populations to side with him. What had not been possible on the Peninsula might be over the Strait of Messina.

Sicily at the end of the seventies was a difficult territory for the Romans, at least from the point of view of public order: "The dangers of a servile war had been envisaged by the provisions of the praetors no less than by the discipline of the masters," writes Cicero, who in *The Verrine Orations* gives us an effective sketch of a situation at risk, with recurrent episodes of insubordination and resistance from Lilybaeum to Panormus to Henna. Even a Roman citizen, a certain Publius Gavius, mistaken for a slave, was accused of spying for Spartacus and put to death.

The quality of administration was generally poor, due to incompetence and corruption, in a sleazy mix of politics and business. The big servile and plebeian revolts of the previous decades had left dangerous hotbeds, which had never been entirely extinguished, and the conditions of the servile masses—exploited to the very limits of survival—had not significantly improved on the *latifundia* and *villae,* and the same could be said for the rural plebs. Discontent was growing in the cities as well, exacerbated by the arrogance of the wealthier groups.

Spartacus was indubitably aware of the situation, and probably really did have spies and infiltrators out in the field, not just slaves, ready to move into action. We should not be surprised. At the peak of his success, he had a network of informers without which his movements and victories would have been unthinkable. Perhaps the vastness of these contacts also led him to believe the revolt might spread.

His plan envisaged various stages. Initially, just two thousand men were to land in Sicily, with the task of stirring up the insurrection again, at least in the eastern part of the island. Once secure bridgeheads had been established, the rest of his army—which in the meantime would keep Crassus's forces at bay—would move to take the whole island.

There was, however, the sea to cross, the dangerous strait meticulously described by Sallust. Spartacus's first idea was to find ships. In the preceding months he had had contacts with groups of pirates, who infested the Mediterranean in those years, especially toward the east, and were bold enough to make forays along the Italian coastline, plundering or selling booty and slaves seized all over the place. In 75, some of them had even captured the young Caesar, holding him hostage for several weeks, while in 72 (we do not know exactly when), a small flotilla commanded by a man named Heracleon (Pyrganion, according to Orosius) had not hesitated to break into the port of Syracusae. In the same months a Roman squadron was in Crete—one of the pirates' best-equipped hideouts—in an effort to block the continual incursions.

And it was to pirates that Spartacus now turned for assistance. The ones he approached were from Cilicia, a coastal region in the south of Asia Minor, and they might have had a number of reasons for helping the rebels: Rome was a common enemy. Agreement was reached, and many gifts were handed over in exchange for passage across the strait—not, then, real payment as such, perhaps in keeping with ancient Mediterranean customs.

The Romans in Sicily were expecting a landing, and the governor, who had no significant garrisons, tried nonetheless to prepare defenses. His name was Gaius Verres, later to become famous for a trial in which Cicero delivered some celebrated orations against him. In these circumstances, the orator had every interest to belittle the importance of the measures adopted by Verres, in order to emphasize his corrupt ineptitude. But Sallust tells us that the magistrate fortified the coastline facing Italy. And steps certainly were taken in the autumn, a sign that the imminence and gravity of the danger could not be underestimated by anyone, not even by someone like Verres. Far from being a man in flight, Spartacus was still considered a threatening invader.

Then, unexpectedly, Spartacus's plan went awry, and the pirates "betrayed him and sailed away"—

perhaps because of a last-minute dispute, possibly dissuaded following contacts with the Romans, or maybe just frightened by the proportions of the endeavor.

We do not know how many ships the pirates had promised to supply. It is possible there were not enough even for the first contingent Spartacus planned to ferry over, and that he had to think from the outset of an alternative solution: the building of rafts, which now, after the defection, were the only means of attempting a crossing. In fact he immediately set about constructing them—a naval engineering task that was not, moreover, just the fruit of hurried improvisation. In 250, in the course of the First Punic War, Lucius Cecilius Metellus had brought captured Carthaginian elephants back to Italy in much the same way. Wooden staves were placed on top of empty casks and large earthenware jars, and lashed together with strips of leather or vine withies, recount Sallust and Florus (vines again, like that night on Vesuvius, where everything had begun!). At any rate, the craft—some at least—were launched. Probably the stretch of sea chosen for the crossing was between Cape Cenide, now Punta Pezzo (the Via Annia, descending from the Aspromonte, ended nearby) and Cape Peloro, on the Sicilian coast, a short and fairly easy route ending up at a point before the mountain chain extending toward Catania—a fragment of Sallust leads us to suppose so. Sicily was just a short hop away, clearly visible from the point Spartacus had chosen. Pliny calculated little more than two kilometers, Strabo even less, but the shape of the terrain is very different today, and the distance is greater, just over three kilometers (if, of course, the ancient authors were not mistaken).

The waters of the strait were very rough (they always are at that point), the currents strong, and it was late autumn. High waves swept in and broke unremittingly on the beach. What's more, Spartacus's men would have been anything but seasoned mariners. Another brief fragment of Sallust captures a dramatic image: "the rafts got caught up in each other, preventing them from maneuvering." It was a complete fiasco. Quite a few of the rebels might have drowned, and arms and equipment were certainly lost. The plan was aborted: Sicily could wait. There was no way out of Italy in that direction.

· 8 ·

Crassus, from a safe distance, stood by and watched. I would rule out that he contributed, as Cicero claims, to the failure of the operation, or that he pursued Spartacus almost down to the beach. When Cicero was writing, in 70, he had every reason to speak highly of him and tried in every way to denigrate Verres. Crassus must hardly have believed his luck: he had finally pushed the enemy into the furthest corner of Italy, almost without fighting, after the rebels, maneuvering brilliantly, had covered thousands of kilometers in the previous two years. And while Spartacus, having abandoned the coast and bypassed Rhegium (today's Reggio Calabria), moved northward again across the Aspromonte, the Roman commander came up with the idea of consolidating the result with a hair-brained operation of rare strategic clumsiness. He ordered the construction of a wall from coast to coast, between the Tyrrhenian and the Ionian, at the point where the Italic Peninsula narrows and just a thin isthmus separates the two seas, either between Sant'Eufemia and the Gulf of Squillace, or—a better hypothesis—more or less along the line of the state road now linking Locri and Gioia Tauro (in this case the distance calculated by Plutarch would correspond more closely). At any rate, the intent was to hem in Spartacus's army—and his formidable cavalry—against difficult mountainous terrain.

The decision crudely reveals Crassus's insecurity and lack of skill. The last thing he wanted was a pitched, fully deployed battle with Spartacus. Naturally, he could not hope to guard the whole line of fieldworks in any force (he did not have enough men), nor had he had the time to prepare them really effectively. Plutarch speaks of a ditch stretching three hundred *stadia* (about fifty-five kilometers, which was exactly the width of the isthmus, if the position is the one we have suggested), about fifty *pedes* (Roman feet) deep, and a wall of surprising height and solidity. The ability and efficiency of the Roman sappers were indisputably unique, but it is quite likely that excavations were only made at the points judged to be most readily crossable, perhaps concentrated around the Dorsale Tabulare, or Dossone della Melía, in the far north of the Aspromonte.

In any case Spartacus was not greatly concerned: Plutarch says he "scoffed" at the works. And as soon as he decided an opportune moment had arrived (also because provisions were running low), on "a cold night" of wind and snow—it must have been December or January—he chose a lightly guarded point with just "a small military garrison . . . at that time heedless of the war," filled in a short stretch of ditch in front of him with earth, shrubs, and branches (according to Frontinus, also with animal carcasses and the corpses of prisoners), and in just a few hours got a third of his army across. Crassus, who had senselessly dispersed his forces to guard the useless fortifications (a decision that was necessary at that point, but foolhardy), was in no position to respond. Indeed, he risked being caught in a pincer between the rebel units that had crossed the wall, and that could have attacked from the rear, and those he still had in front. He was therefore constrained to lift the siege, and to pull back toward the north. Spartacus once more had an open road before him.

Crassus feared that the rebels wanted to make for Rome again (so Plutarch says). But it was a nightmare stemming from the humiliation he had suffered, which prevented a cool assessment of the situation. If Spartacus had decided not to attack Rome in the summer, and for very serious reasons, when he was at the height of his success, how could he have thought of doing so now, when nothing had changed to his advantage, he was still getting over the failure to cross the strait, and his men were probably worn down and discouraged?

Here too, we cannot imagine what Spartacus had in mind. Probably he was trying to take account of two contrasting requirements: the need to rest his men, uninterruptedly on the march and in combat since the previous spring; and the necessity to gain a favorable position as quickly as possible, in view of the imminent arrival of Pompey and Lucullus, which could not have escaped him. According to Plutarch, he had thought of withdrawing toward the mountains of Samnium, and this is credible: it had been another place where the Social War had raged.

What is certain is that soon afterward he was in Lucania—it must by now have been February of 71— with Crassus, who in the meantime had reassembled his forces, still intent on maintaining contact. Adopting his customary contingency plan, Spartacus divided up his units, both for logistical reasons and in order to secure better control of the territory and a greater chance of finding new recruits. Plutarch (and, probably, Sallust) hints once more at a disagreement among the rebels, to explain the separation of the columns: but the ensuing events yet again render implausible such a reconstruction.

A strong force of several thousand men had camped by a Lucanian lake known for recurrent changes of its waters, from fresh to salty and back again—possibly a marsh not far from Paestum. Here they were attacked by Crassus, and pushed back from the lake, but were saved by the rapid arrival of Spartacus, who was in the vicinity and had never lost contact (it must, therefore, have been a highly singular split!). In the end, the Romans were repulsed.

It now seemed as if the campaign was going to turn into a long war of attrition. In Rome, many, both among the Optimates and the Populares, opportunely prodded by supporters of Pompey—now back in Italy—began to call for the latter's direct intervention in operations. "Not a few publicly proclaimed that the victory in this war belonged to him." We do not know if the matter reached a formal deliberation, but it is possible the senate was more a spectator than an initiator of the request. Crassus, though he had not long since spoken in favor of such a move, was certainly not happy at the prospect. If Pompey took part in the military actions, the merit for the final victory would be his, and that was not what Crassus wanted at all. So he decided to adopt a more aggressive stance, "having been made only the more eager to hasten the task," Sallust writes.

A large unit of Spartacus's army, led by two commanders, a Celt and a German, Castus and Canicius— possibly the same one that had fought by the lake— had halted in northern Lucania, near Mount Cantenna. Crassus chose to attack in strength before the rebels could join the rest of their forces. The course of the battle, as reported by the Roman tradition, is extremely garbled—a real historical and philological puzzle— but by trying to put some order into the accounts of Frontinus and Plutarch, and in the brief glimpses offered by Sallust, by Orosius, and in Livy's *Periochae*, we can piece together a plausible version.

Crassus had divided his troops into two camps, facing the rebels. In an early phase of the battle, he attempted an encircling maneuver, sending twelve cohorts (about six thousand men) commanded by C. Pomptinus and Q. Marcius Rufus to take up position on a hill behind the enemy's ranks. The ploy might have succeeded had it not been for the intervention of two Celtic women—there were still some, then, with the rebels—who had retired to the summit of a nearby promontory to perform sacrifices (according to Sallust, to be alone while menstruating, considered impure by their religion). In the dim light of dawn, the pair spotted the enemy contingent and cooly raised the alarm. The rebels launched an immediate counterattack, and the Romans "would have come off badly" if Crassus himself had not intervened with the core of his troops to even up the outcome of the day. At this point there was probably a lull, how long we do not know. But by now the two forces were very close to each other. At night, leaving his tent in the most important camp, Crassus moved with his whole army to the bottom of the mountain. Here he divided his cavalry and ordered the legate, Lucius Quinctius, to take some of them and to attack the bulk of Spartacus's army—which must have been in the vicinity, and probably close to joining up with the rest of the rebel troops—in order to keep it away from the main theater of operations.

At this point there was a failure in communications between the Thracian and the two commanders at the head of the other column, and it was to prove decisive. Spartacus, who at that moment did not have adequate cavalry forces, had probably carried out an evasive maneuver taking him away from his secondary group—he was unrivaled in such disengagements—in order to rid himself of the attack by the Roman wing, believing that Castus and Canicius's forces were not in imminent danger. It was a disastrous error of judgment, because the other part of the Roman cavalry had just started to attack them, before then suddenly retreating on the flanks, luring out the Celts and Gauls, who rashly launched a counterattack that took them further and further away from Spartacus's main force, toward the center of Crassus's formation. It was a massacre. At least twelve thousand rebels (the figure of thirty thousand found in Livy's *Periochae* can be discounted) were killed, together with their leaders, while the Roman losses were minimal. The victors also recovered five *fasces lictoriae*, five eagle insignia, and twenty-six battle banners, which the rebels had captured from defeated Roman legions—a tangible symbol of revenge, and at once a demonstration of how hard the rebels had been hit.

A breakdown in communications, and the foolish impetuousity of two commanders, had provoked a catastrophe, while this time Crassus, ably assisted by his officers, had done well, and for once had managed to exploit the tactical automatism of the Roman military machine. Spartacus's main units were still intact, but it had been a terrible blow, and the losses were irreplaceable, at least in the short term. Now the situation really was spiraling out of control.

· 9 ·

Spartacus abandoned the idea of Samnium, which must now have seemed unreacheable, and remained in Lucania, heading toward "the mountains of Petelia." Where these are exactly is unclear; they may be the Picentini Mountains (supposing an error in the text), or the hills of Cilento, southeast of Paestum, or, again, the uplands around Atena Lucana. Crassus, reassured by the victory, stuck closely to Spartacus's heels, sending out his lieutenants, Quintus Marcius Rufus and Cnaeus Tremellius Scrofa, the elected quaester for 71, to explore. But they incautiously moved in too close to the enemy, and Spartacus turned suddenly and attacked, routing them before Crassus had time to bring up his main force. Scrofa himself was injured, and only just managed to escape. It was not a decisive rebel success, but provided some respite.

Spartacus continued to adopt harassing tactics. Once, in the no-man's-land between the two encampments, he had a Roman prisoner crucified "to show his own men what fate awaited them if they did not conquer" (Appian). The brief interlude also gave Spartacus time for a further gambit, political this time and not military: he tried to open negotiations with Crassus. It was a surprising step. Why did he make it and what did he hope to obtain?

The gravity of the situation was quite evident. Pompey was in Etruria, and liable to enter the fray at any moment with overwhelming forces. By now it was hard enough dealing just with Crassus; with the arrival of the other army, all would be lost. But Spartacus was aware of the rivalry between the two Roman commanders, and the bitterness of the political infighting in Rome. By trying to negotiate, he hoped to open up a breach in the enemy front, which he could then exploit with some prospect of success. Hannibal had done much the same in his own time.

Spartacus's ploy was chiefly a bid for legitimation: if Crassus agreed to negotiate, the rebels would finally be considered an invading army, and not a band (albeit very large!) of slaves. And he himself would be treated as the general of a foreign people, who was appealing, with due right, to Roman *fides* (Tacitus), a word charged with history and significance—the commitment to respect based on reciprocity. And this, as we have seen, had always been Spartacus's main political goal: to dilute the servile origins of the revolt in a wider movement, a more general Italic uprising against Rome, led by an army of Thracians, Celts, and Germans.

Even though he had not managed to defeat the Romans, he wanted at least to be their interlocutor. To finally enter the political arena.

It was a tardy and, in a sense, desperate move. But above all, Spartacus failed to take account of the fact that the image he had been cultivating of himself—a military commander at the head of an army which had covered itself with glory—did not coincide with the one the Romans had of him. For them, he was still just a rebel slave. In the blindness of the prejudice, nothing else counted. Caesar alone would refer to Spartacus's forces as an army of barbarians rather than of slaves. He was however talking as a soldier (we cannot entirely rule out in his reference an implicit tribute to the brilliant rebel commander) and not as a politician, far less as a master.

Nothing came of it. Crassus rejected the proposal contemptuously, and tightened his grip, managing to block the path of the enemy army with fortified fieldworks (his favorite way of operating). But Spartacus succeeded yet again in breaking the blockade, and seemingly made for Apulia, toward Brundisium, not because he was thinking of taking ship for Thrace, as has sometimes been suggested—and with what means, if he had not even been able to cross the Strait of Messina?—but as a final attempt to gain time and space, and to return to an area where he could perhaps still count on finding some support. But the news that Lucullus had just landed there from Macedonia made him desist. Signs of restlessness and disbandment might also have been appearing in his ranks. Plutarch mentions it, probably drawing on Sallust, and this time, given the circumstances, he seems reliable. The stress his men were under, after a year in combat, was immense, and the discipline they had been subjected to, though it had performed miracles, could well have slipped at times.

Spartacus therefore had no choice but to fight his final battle—at least still against Crassus alone, before Pompey and perhaps even Lucullus were upon him.

It was the end of March, or April, of 71, the beginning of spring, and we do not know exactly where Spartacus was. One reliable hypothesis has him in the upper reaches of the Sele Valley, on a fairly extensive plain not far from the town of Civita, in the far south of today's province of Salerno.

Shortly before, there had been skirmishes between rebel scouts and Roman patrols guarding the ditches Crassus had ordered to be dug. Spartacus, who had rebuilt his cavalry (what he had lacked in the unfortunate episode of Castus and Canicius), drew up his army. From a numerical point of view, the opposing forces were almost equivalent, with perhaps a slight advantage for the Romans: neither of the two commanders could count on more than forty-five to fifty thousand men. The same could not be said about the logistics, equipment, and physical and mental condition of the combatants. Here the Roman superiority was crushing. Spartacus undoubtedly had a plan: he would have tried to maneuver his cavalry on a flank—perhaps the one furthest from the river—despite the ditches, in an effort to lure out the center of the Roman army, consisting mainly of light infantry, to then envelop them from his wings.

What is most striking, however, is that the Roman tradition, gathered by Plutarch, reports that from the outset he wanted to turn the battle into a personal clash—a kind of duel—between himself and Crassus. Before moving, reports Plutarch, drawing on Sallust, Spartacus slew his horse—a sacred animal in the Thracian religion—probably in a ritual consecrating himself definitively to Dionysius. He then reputedly declared (and these are the only words directly attributed to him in all the Roman accounts we know of) that "if he won the day he would have many fine horses of the enemy's, but if he lost it he would no longer need any." After which he plunged into the fray in search of Crassus.

But we must be careful; with this story we are departing from the history of the war and the account of a single battle. We are already into the legend of

Spartacus—a legend of the people, and not just of slaves, we must assume, otherwise Sallust would not have recorded it—which formed immediately after the events.

And indeed we are unable to reconstruct a single maneuver of the battle. All we know is that it was long and terrible. The eyes of memory—I repeat, not just of servile memory—are all focussed on the protagonist, mesmorized by his figure, and by that alone.

Spartacus, so the story goes, fought in the front rank, "primo agmine." He killed two centurions who attacked him simultaneously. He did not find Crassus. And here the narrative machine produces two versions. One was that Spartacus was wounded in the thigh by a javelin. Falling to his knees, he discarded his shield and continued to fight off assailants. Finally, he died, surrounded by a large number of his men. The other is that he fought but his army began to break up around him. He ended up on his own. Encircled by a throng of enemies, he was slain while defending himself, still standing. The first scene is choral, the second centers more on the protagonist. In both, his end is represented according to the Roman model of great military virtue: Spartacus fell "quasi imperator," writes Florus, "like a victorious commander." While Sallust, more soberly but with equal respect, says: "He met his death while defending himself vigorously, and selling his life dearly." A Roman fresco found in a house in Pompeii in 1927, and datable to around the middle of the first century, appears to tally with the second version, if the image really does refer to Spartacus, as is seemingly indicated by some Oscan words in the painting, and as I consider fairly likely. If this were the case, it would be a further clue that the legend spread immediately, and that its narrative engine developed some very popular images—a kind of Spartacus iconography—destined to adorn the houses of the rich, besides more erudite writings, conserved in their libraries.

Appian relates that Spartacus's body was never found—and thus escaped defilement. It is another element of the legend, leaving scope for all kinds of tales of transfiguration and immortality. His feats had all been performed under the aura of a charisma suffused with strong prophetic and religious overtones. The disappearance of his corpse consigns the conclusion of the story to the indecipherable, shadowy mysteries, between life and death, the human and the divine, where everything became possible.

And his companion? We have just seen that even in the final weeks there were women with the rebels. So we can presume that the priestess of Dionysius accompanied Spartacus to the end. We know nothing more about her: Was she killed? But she might also have managed to escape. Perhaps she had a child. We would like to leave her in this way—as in Kubrick's movie—free and in the company of trusted brigands in the impenetrable forests between the Sila Plateau and the Aspromonte. After all, why not?

At any rate, the battle ended in a slaughter. Thousands and thousands of rebels died, even though the figure of sixty thousand found in Livy's *Periochae* is not credible. The Romans lost a thousand men. The roundup started straight away. Crassus ventured into the nearby mountains in pursuit of some of the fugitives, who, grouped in four columns, put up stiff resistance. Many others, who had taken the road north, were intercepted by Pompey on his way down from Etruria. But many succeeded in slipping through the net cast by the Roman troops, and ended up joining bands of outlaws or bandits, or the microrevolts dotted around almost endemically in the open expanses of southern Italy. Of these men, all trace has naturally been lost. History closed in over them.

Six thousand prisoners were "crucified along the whole road from Capua to Rome," almost certainly the Appian Way. Never before had there been such mass executions in the Roman world. The road, about two hundred kilometers long, was flanked on both sides by the bodies of the victims and by their executioners. Picturing that forest of crosses on the outskirts of Rome is shocking for us, and not just, obviously, because of the unprecedented massacre. But at that time, those nailed timbers were still just a cheap and efficient instrument of torture and death, nothing more than an "extreme" and "terrible" way of dealing with rebel slaves.

A small group of Spartacus's men did remain together, though, and continued to fight for a long time. In fact, they were still active ten years later, in 60. And once more we find them in the countryside around Thurii, which they had occupied yet again.

They were not alone.

With them were the survivors of the army of Catiline, who had also met a valiant end, weapons in hand, near Pistoria (Pistoia), in January of 62: "refugees from

the armies of Spartacus and Catiline," writes Suetonius. The subterranean thread connecting the two insurrections surfaced now just to link together their
miserable remnants—fragments adrift from a history
that had not come to be.

It was the lot of the new governor of Macedonia, a
former praetor, and a capable and reliable politician, to
be chosen by the senate, before taking office in his
province, to finish the work of Crassus and of Marcus
Petreius (who had defeated Catiline), and to extin-
guish with blood that last hotbed of resistance. His
name was Gaius Octavius—and he had just recently
become the father of a child, Octavianus, later known
as Augustus.

The truth of history often likes to conceal itself in
small coincidences.

· 10 ·

Spartacus's insurrection closed the cycle of the great
slave revolts in the history of Rome. No subsequent episode would ever be anything more than an isolated,
local incident with solely marginal consequences.

The crisis of the institutions and of the ruling groups,
though, would continue for much longer—forty years
after the death of Spartacus, and thirty after that of
Catiline, and would involve at least another two gen-
erations. The political change—it is inappropriate to
call it, as many people do, a "revolution"—eventually
arrived in the only way possible in that situation. Not
through a rupture featuring the plebeian core of the

republic; nothing even remotely comparable to a democratic revolution. But via the ambiguous path of a coup d'état—that of Augustus—arising from within the old senatorial nobility itself, or at least a part of it. It was a cautious solution in appearance but radically innovative in substance, which adapted, without excessive cultural and institutional rifts (a further instance of the Romans' fear of the new), the form of government to the needs and dimensions of a world primacy, and enlarged, albeit prudently and with great care, the social base of the dominant orders to include the Romanized elites of the whole empire. Rome opened up toward the world, rather than identifying just with Italy. The ancient oligarchy, heir to the glories of the republic, surrendered some of its exclusivism and privileges, but in exchange was able to conserve some measure of its power.

The new constitutional setup, an autocracy with a number of checks and balances centering on the new figure of the emperor *(princeps),* helped to achieve great political, cultural, and social stabilization. Moderate and neo-aristocratic in nature—and praised by Virgil and Horace—it would last, albeit with increasing concessions to the army and its chiefs, for about two centuries. After so much perturbation, the frightful *res novae* dissolved without trace, and the tensions of the late-republican age were absorbed and sterilized by the passiveness of a plebeian base (it is hard to describe it as "popular") that the permanent distance from productive labor, and the consequent lack of class structures, pushed toward immobility and resignation. The urban plebs lost political significance, but in return at least had the wherewithal to feed themselves with a certain regularity.

It is impossible to say whether it would ever have been possible to emerge in any other way from the storm that raged in the republican order for a century. History does not allow such verification. In the years running from the Gracchi to Caesar, during the most tumultuous and feverish period of growth, something different did dimly appear, closer to what we would describe as "modern," before breaking up immediately against the profound limits of that society. Spartacus was a figure who stood in this deceptive light. The imperial order earned centuries of life, but closed off any paths that might have opened up equilibria different from those of a very protracted stagnation.

The neo-aristocratic stabilization was accompanied by a no less imposing stabilization of the slave system, thereby consolidating its dual and contradictory nature as an indispensable requirement for maintaining the levels of intellectual and material life achieved by that society, and at the same time as an insuperable barrier to any further development. It underpinned that world and yet thwarted it.

The terrible coercion that relentlessly accompanied the existence of millions of slaves was never substantively eased, nor was the ferocious discipline to which they were subjected. A measure introduced at the behest of Augustus himself reaffirmed that in the event of the homicide of a master, all the slaves living "under the same roof" as him were to be tortured and put to death, because, as a great jurist would explain two centuries later, "no house could otherwise ever have been safe, if not by obliging slaves, on pain of death, to defend their master both from dangers arising within his home and from without." In A.D. 61, the intransigent application of this norm, despite the disguised opposition of the emperor himself—Nero—would lead to the summary execution, in the heart of Rome, of four hundred slaves, including many women and children.

But such ruthlessness did not prevent a great many slaves, especially in the cities—millions probably, in the course of Rome's history, both men and women—from becoming integrated into imperial society, and not just at the lowest levels, and from being accepted not as an extraneous body but as an active and vital element. Revealed in this tendency is the extraordinary Roman talent—as yet unequaled in world history—for the unprejudiced assimilation of different cultures and peoples, provided they participated in some way in the great processes of unifying the empire. One of the most important methods of this absorption took the form of manumissions. Through them, every single master, without any intervention from the political authorities, could give a slave his liberty, making him a freedman *(libertus)*. This at the same time granted him Roman citizenship (it seems incredible, but has a precise historical explanation). In the final decades of the republic, the practice became extremely widespread. Many masters preferred to have free citizens bound to them by legal and economic obligations, as freedmen were, rather than elderly slaves who had to be maintained. And it was Augustus, once again, who had to establish that no more than one hundred slaves could be manumitted in a will, though he left it to the master's discretion as to how many to free while he was alive. In Rome in those years, hundreds of thousands of citizens had servile origins. Later, in the age of Nero, there was talk in the senate, according to Tacitus, that the majority of knights, not to mention many of the senators themselves, had some blood deriving from a freedman. And a not inconsiderable contribution was also made by the jurists, who effectively permitted more able slaves to create their own patrimonies, with which to buy their freedom.

So there took shape an elastic and multiform space of cultural intertwinings, of social practices and power, of relations and exchanges, shared by the world of the free and by that of the slaves. I believe it is in precisely these circuits that the story of Spartacus became collective memory, quickly incorporating segments of legend arising soon after the death of a "hero" who grasped a weapon to the very end: in a word, like a true . . . Roman warrior.

THE ANCIENT SOURCES

What has come down to us of the ancient stories about the Spartacus war—about the "scandal" of those events—raises highly complex interpretative problems. The most important and extensive accounts available to us are those of Plutarch in his "Life of Crassus," 8–11 [Lindskog-Ziegler], and of Appian in the first book of the *The Civil Wars*, 116,539–120,559 [Vierek-Roos-Gabba]. In all, they do not even amount to ten pages in length, and are readily consultable in English in the editions of the Loeb Classical Library: Plutarch in *Plutarch's Lives*, 10 vols., translated by B. Perrin (Cambridge, Mass., 1916; reprint 1958), vol. 3, pp. 335–351; and Appian in *Appian's Roman History*, 4 vols., translated by H. White (Cambridge, Mass., 1913; reprint 1964), vol. 3, pp. 215–225. All the citations of the two authors, unless otherwise specified, are taken from these two blocks of text. In some cases, the translations have been modified.

Plutarch was writing in the decades following A.D. 100, Appian just a bit later, around the middle of the second century—a long time after the reported events. Their narratives do not overlap, except in very broad terms. They were the result of different historiographic selections and expository choices, with respect to a tradition that had evidently already formed on the theme. But who did it lead back to? And was it a univocal version, or were there different judgments and accounts of the Spartacus story in circulation? And how was this material used by the two writers? Almost all the problems raised by modern criticism revolve around these questions. But there is no point trying to unravel the tangle here; the reconstruction offered in the book is itself what, in my view, is the most convincing and plausible answer.

We are at any rate certain that at the beginning of every ancient historiographic elaboration on this subject there must have been Sallust and Livy: the historiography about Spartacus starts with them. But of the Sallustian account, in the third and fourth books of the *Histories,* composed between 39 and 35, just a small group of fragments remains: 3,90–106; 4,20–41 (also 5,1–2), and perhaps two very short ones of uncertain placement: 4 and 20 [Maurenbrecher] (see also L. Reynolds [ed.], *Sallust Catalina, Iugurtha, Historiarum Fragmenta Selecta; Appendix Sallustiana* [Oxford, 1991]), which can be read in English in Sallust, *The Histories,* 2 vols., translated, with an introduction and commentary, by P. McGushin (Oxford, 1994), vol. 2, pp. 23–52. Even less can be related to Livy: three brief texts of the *Periochae* (a summary of Livian contents not without textual contaminations, prepared, possibly in the fourth century A.D., by an unknown compiler working from an earlier epitome): 95–97 [Rossbach].

We do, however, have three other sources of some substance: a passage from the second book of the *Epitome* by Lucius Annaeus Florus, a historian working in the Trajan era, who, though certainly familiar with Livy, had some knowledge of Sallust as well: 2,8 [Jal], English translation by E. S. Forster, *Epitome of Roman History* (Cambridge, Mass., 1929; 7th ed. 1984), pp. 240–245; a brief series of four texts by Frontinus—an expert in hydraulic technology and military matters, who also lived between the end of the first and the beginning of the second century A.D.— from his *Stratagems:* 1,5,20–22; 1,7,6; 2,4,7; 2,5,34 [Gundermann]; and finally, two sizable passages from Orosius—a pupil of Augustine, and the author of the *Historiae adversus paganos,* who drew on Livy, Tacitus, Justin, and Eusebius—5,22,5–8 and 5,24,1–

10 [Zangemeister], English translation by A. T. Fear, *Seven Books of History against the Pagans* (Liverpool, 2010), pp. 253 and 258–259.

In addition we have other shorter, more fleeting yet at times invaluable pieces of testimony, in particular of Caesar, Cicero, Varro, Diodorus of Sicily, Velleius Paterculus, Pliny, Tacitus, Suetonius, and Ampelius (disregarding a few less important ones). Many of them are mentioned in the course of the book, and more specific references are given in the notes as they arise.

NOTES

Chapter 1: The Fugitive

Sec. 1, pp. 1–4

The Florus reference is in 2,8,4. Recently, L. Chioffi, "Tifata, Spartacus e Vesuvius," in M. L. Chirico and L. Chioffi (eds.), *Lungo l'Appia. Scritti su Capua antica e dintorni* (Naples, 2009), has suggested a different location, presenting some interesting arguments, but I prefer to remain faithful to tradition. Apart from Plutarch and Appian, see also Frontinus, *Strat.* 1,5,21; Florus, *Ep.* 2,8,4; Orosius, *Hist.* 5,24,1.

The two references to Frontinus are in *Strat.* 1,5,21.

The Cicero citation is from *De lege agraria* 2,91 (but see also 2,93). On Vesuvian wines, see A. Tchernia, *Le vin de l'Italie romaine* (Rome, 1986), pp. 49–50, 176–177, 240–241. A fine essay is M. Frederiksen, "I cambiamenti delle strutture agrarie nella tarda repubblica: la Campania," in A. Giardina and A. Schiavone (eds.), *Società romana e produzione schiavistica*, vol. 1 (Rome, 1981), pp. 265ff.

The reference to Frontinus is in *Strat.* 1,5,21.

Claudius Glaber was praetor in that year, according to T. R. S. Broughton, *The Magistrates of the Roman Republic*, 3 vols.

(Cleveland, Ohio; reprint 1968), vol. 2, p. 109. For more about his identification, see G. Stampacchia, *La tradizione della guerra di Spartaco da Sallustio a Orosio* (Pisa, 1976), pp. 25–26.

The number of fugitives involved is considered by Stampacchia, *La tradizione della guerra di Spartaco*, pp. 22–23.

Sec. 2, pp. 4–7

The Cicero citations are from *De lege agraria*, 2,97; 2,91 (see also 2,86); 2,95; 2,96.

Capua was already a city of slaves in the third century: Livy 24,19,2; 26,24,1. The case of Delos is reported by Strabo, 14,5,2 [Meineke].

"A municipal regulation": *Ann. Epigr.*, 1961, 88 (Bove) = *Ann. Epigr.*, 2003, 336 (Hinard and Dumont) = *Ann. Epigr.*, 2004, 421 (Camodeca, Bodel, et al.); C. Dumont, *Servus. Rome et l'esclavage sous la république* (Rome, 1987), pp. 126ff.; and Y. Thomas, "Vitae necisque potestas: Le père, la cité, la mort," in Y. Thomas (ed.), *Du châtiment dans la cité: Supplice corporels et peine de mort dans le monde antique* (Rome, 1984), pp. 499ff.

Caesar's jurist friend was Aulus Ofilius. We know about the definition, probably formulated in his books *ad edictum*, from Ulpian, in *Digesta* 21.1.17pr.

The line of verse by Juvenal is in *Sat.* 10,81.

Sec. 3, pp. 7–12

Caesar's school is mentioned by Cicero, *Ad Att.* 7,14.

Livy's recollection is in 9,40,17.

For more about the buildings in Pompeii, see B. Strauss, *The Spartacus War* (New York, 2009), p. 23.

On the name of Lentulus Batiatus, see Stampacchia, *La tradizione della guerra di Spartaco*, pp. 16–17. An idea of what the gladiator shows were like in Rome can be gained from E. Teyssier, *La mort en face: Le dossier Gladiateurs* (Arles, 2009).

The citation from Valerius Maximus is in 2,4,7.

The information about the games of 183 is in Livy 39,46,2.

The Varro citation is from *De lingua lat.* 6,3,12: A. Schiavone, "Dodici Tavole e 'ortodossia' repubblicana," in J.-L. Ferrary (ed.), *Leges publicae: La legge nell'esperienza giuridica romana* (Pavia, 2012), pp. 293ff., especially pp. 298ff.; and Schiavone, *The Invention of Law in the West,* translated by J. Carden and A. Shugaar (Cambridge, Mass., 2012), pp. 59ff.

The citation from Polybius is in 6,56,6–15.

The "martial state of soul" is a citation from J. Hillman, *A Terrible Love of War* (New York, 2004), p. 1.

The citation of Terence refers to *Hecyr.* 39–41.

The citation of Artemidorus is from *onirocriticon* [Pack], 2,32; in English as *The Interpretation of Dreams,* translated by R. J. White (Park Ridge, N.J., 1975), p. 111.

Sec. 4, pp. 12–15

The Cicero citation is from *Tusc.* 2,17,41.

The Sallust citation is from *Hist.* 4,69, 20.

The second citation from Artemidorus is also in 2,32; *Interpretation of Dreams,* p. 111.

Spartacus is described as a *murmillo* by Florus, 2,8,12.

Sec. 5, pp. 15–22

The Florus citation is in 2,8,8. The text from the *Phillipics* is in 4,6,15. The second citation from Florus is from 2,8,9.

The Varro citation is in *Varr. Apud Char. gramm.,* 1,133 [Keil].

"and perhaps in Posidonius": as found in Diodorus (the dependence of Diodorus on Posidonius seems to be indisputable here); see L. Canfora, "La rivolta dei dannati della terra," in Diodorus, *La rivolta degli schiavi in Sicilia* (Palermo, 1983), pp. 51ff.

" 'tributary' instead of 'mercenary' ": the term is well translated by P. Jal (ed.), in Florus, *Oeuvres,* 2 vols. (Paris, reprint 2002), vol. 2, p. 22.

The citation from Herodotus is from 5,3,1. The reference to Thucydides is in 2, 95–101.

The alternatives are "Maidikou" and "nomadikou," in 8,3. Here I follow K. Ziegler's proposal in the Teubner edition of Plutarch, *Plut. Vitae,* vol. 1, fasc. 2 (Leipzig, 1964), p. 136.

The fragment of Sallust is in 3,91.

"praotēs": 8,3; *tychē* and *ghenos,* also in 8,3.

"Epigraphic evidence": A. Passerini, under the entry "Legio," in *Dizionario epigrafico di antichità romane* (Rome, reprint 1942), p. 553.

Sec. 6, pp. 23–27

"There are those who believe Spartacus was already in Italy in 83": for example, E. Gabba, in *Appiani Bellorum civilium* (Florence, 1958), p. 317 (note).

Sec. 7, pp. 27–31

A fine book about Dionysius—a genuine classic—is C. Kerényi, *Dionysos: Urbild des unzerstörbaren Lebens* (Munich, reprint 1976); in English as *Dionysos: Archetypal Image of Indestructible Life,* translated by R. Manheim (Princeton, N.J., 1976). See also F. Frontisi-Ducroux, "Dioniso e il suo culto," in S. Settis (ed.), *I Greci: Storia, Cultura, Arte, Società,* 4 vols. (Turin, 1996–2004), vol. 2, bk. 2, pp. 275ff., and, more particularly, P. Piccinin, "Le dionysisme dans le 'Bellum Spartacium,'" *La parola del passato* 56 (2001), pp. 272ff.

The Greek words cited are in 8,4. The Greek words cited in relation to the uncertainty of reading are also in 8,4.

The Columella citation is from *Res rust.* 3,3,8. For more, see R. Duncan Jones, *The Economy of the Roman Empire: Quantitative Studies,* 2nd ed. (Cambridge, U.K., 1982), pp. 39–40, 348ff.

The cost of the grammarian slave is mentioned by Pliny in *Nat. hist.* 7,40,128.

Sec. 8, pp. 31–35

"graffiti found in Pompeii": L. Jacobelli, *Gladiators at Pompeii* (Rome, 2003), pp. 48–49, 65–66.

"a slight discordance": Stampacchia, *La tradizione della guerra di Spartaco,* pp. 16–17.

"probably on a route parallel to the Via Annia": T. P. Wiseman, "Viae Anniae," in *Papers of the British School at Rome* 32 (1964), pp. 21ff.

Sec. 9, pp. 35–38

"*asmenoi*": 9,1.

"*ypostrategoi*": 116, 540. Florus: 8,3. Orosius: 24,1. On the question of who was in command, see Stampacchia, *La tradizione della guerra di Spartaco*, pp. 17ff.

"already virtually as bandits": A. Giardina, "Uomini e spazi aperti," in *L'Italia romana: Storie di un'identità incompiuta* (Rome, 1997), pp. 193ff. See also B. D. Shaw, "Bandits in the Roman Empire," *Past and Present* 105 (1984), pp. 3ff.

CHAPTER 2: THE COMMANDER

Sec. 1, pp. 39–44

"revenge": 8.3.

"Florus says … ": 8.3.

"As Andrea Giardina has noted": in A. Giardina, "Uomini e spazi aperti," in *L'Italia romana: Storie di un'identità incompiuta* (Rome, 1997), p. 202.

"Appian carefully specifies": 116,540.

Sec. 2, pp. 44–52

"remembered by Frontinus": 1,5,22; cf. Livy, *Per.* 95; T. R. S. Broughton, *The Magistrates of the Roman Republic*, 3 vols. (Cleveland, Ohio; reprint 1968), vol. 2, p. 110.

"praetor in 75": Broughton, *The Magistrates*, vol. 2, pp. 97 and 112.

"who got it from Sallust": *Hist.*, 3.94.

"fragment 95": unless, that is, we reconsider the position of the fragment in the book, moving it further forward. In this case it could refer to a much bigger battle (see pp. 51–52).

"heavy autumn": 3,96A.

"rampart, ditch, and extensive earthworks": 3,96B.

"by Frontinus": 1,5,22.

"Sallust is severe in his judgment": "contra spectatam rem incaute motus": 3,96D.

"Sallust reports": 3,96D.

"Sallust's account": though it might be possible to position the above-mentioned fragment 95 here.

"as we learn from Florus": 2,8,5.

Sec. 3, pp. 52–57

"memories of his native land": "patriae immemores," writes Sallust in 3,98A.

"to leave as quickly as possible": 3,98A.

"reported by Florus": 2,8,5.

"Sallust claims": 3,98A–B.

"increase their number with select recruits": 3,98B.

Antisthenes of Rhodes: FGrHist 257F 36 (the citation is from 3,9), mediated through Phlegon of Tralles. The man who had the prophetic dream was Publius Cornelius Scipio Africanus: J.-L. Ferrary, *Philhellénisme et imperialisme: Aspects idéologiques de la conquête romaine du monde hellénistique, de la seconde guerre de Macédoine à la guerre contre Mithridate* (Rome, 1988), pp. 238ff., 362.

Sec. 4, pp. 57–61

"surprising the peasants": Sallust, 3,98B–C.

"barbarous rage and a servile nature": 3,98C.

"hatred": 3,98D.

"divided the plunder": Appian, 116,541.

"he prohibited": Appian, 117,547.

"is reported by Pliny as well": *Nat. hist.* 33,14,49–50.

"rural communitarianism": important observations can be found in A. Giardina, "Allevamento ed economia della selva in Italia meridionale," in *L'Italia romana,* pp. 138ff., especially 142ff.

"Sallust would write": *Bellum Iugurthinum* 8,1.

"to 'beg' his men": Sallust, 3,98C.

Sec. 5, pp. 61–63

"in a fairly spacious level area": Sallust, 3,98D.

"Sallust reports": 3,98D.

"saved by Sallust": 3,99.

"we read in Sallust": 3,100.
"writes Florus": 2,8,5.

Sec. 6, pp. 63–66
"the definition of Varro": *Res rust.* 1,17,1; the Aristotelian reference is to the *Politics,* 1,4 (1253b) and to the *Nicomachean Ethics,* 8,11 (1161b).
"as recounted by Plutarch": *Tiberius Gracchus,* 8–9 = *ORF,* 4th ed., 13–15 (the subsequent citation is also from the same source).
"Diodorus writes": 34–35,2,27 [Walton], but see also 2,1. The citations of Diodorus's work are from *Diodorus of Sicily,* 12 vols., translated by F. Walton (Cambridge, Mass., 1967), vol. 12. In some cases, the translations have been modified.

Sec. 7, pp. 66–70
"recorded by Livy": 33,26,4–18 (but also *Periochae,* 32 and Zonaras, 9,16,6); 33,36,13. Also to be borne in mind: 32,26,4–18; 39,29,8–9; 39,41,6–7. A useful study is M. Capozza, *Movimenti servili nel mondo romano in età repubblicana,* vol. 1, *Dal 501 al 184 A.C.* (Rome, 1966), pp. 101ff. and 121ff.
"the comedies of Plautus": this is immediately apparent from a reading of *Rudens* or the *Pseudolus.*
"slave in charge of his personal library": *Ad fam.* 13,77,3.

Sec. 8, pp. 70–78
"The herdsmen": Diodorus, 34–35,2,29 (but see also 2,27–28).
"There was never a sedition of slaves so great": Diodorus, 34–35, 2,25–26.
"an immense number": Diodorus, 34–35, 2, 27.
"Many serious troubles befell the Sicilians": Diodorus, 34–35, 2,48.
"Diodorus presents him": 34–35,2,4–9.
"All this time the poor slaves": Seneca, *Ep. ad Luc.,* 5,47,3.
"as we learn from Athenaeus": 6,88–90, 265d–266e (Kaibel): K. R. Bradley, *Slavery and Rebellion in the Roman World, 140 B.C.–70 B.C.* (Bloomington, Ind., 1989), pp. 38ff. On marronage, see: I. Berlin, *Many Thousands Gone: The First Two Centuries of Slavery*

in *North America* (Cambridge, Mass., 1998), pp. 87–88, 120ff., 169–170, 305–306, 328–329, 339–340; R. Price, "Maroons and their Communities," in G. Heuman and J. Walvin (eds.), *The Slavery Reader* (London, 2003), pp. 608ff.; O. Pétré-Grenouilleau, *Dictionnaire des esclavages* (Paris, 2010), pp. 465ff. Although the term "trade" was first used in reference to the modern Atlantic slave trade in black slaves—a now classic study is H. Thomas, *The Slave Trade: The Story of the Atlantic Slave Trade, 1440–1870* (New York, 1999), but see also O. Pétré-Grenouilleau, *Les Traits négrières: Essai d'histoire globale* (Paris, 2004)—in this book I have decided to use it for imperial Roman slavery as well.

"Diodorus, again, tells us": 34–35,2,28. In Livy, *Periochae* 56, the figure is seventy thousand: P. Green, "The First Sicilian Slave War," *Past and Present* 20 (1961), pp. 10ff.; G. P. Verbrugghe, "Slave Rebellion or Sicily in Revolt?" *Kokalos* 20 (1974), pp. 46ff.; A. Fraschetti, "Per una prosopografia dello sfruttamento: romani e italici in Sicilia (212–44 A.C.)," in A. Giardina and A. Schiavone (eds.), *Società romana e produzione schiavistica*, vol. 1 (Rome, 1981), pp. 53ff.

"According to Appian": *Bell. civ.* I,9,35–37.

"Diodorus recounts": 34–35,2,46.

"for Diodorus": the full account of the episode is in 36,2,1–6.

"who was reputed to be skilled in divination": Diodorus, 36,4,4.

"those without means": Diodorus, 36,6.

Sec. 9, pp. 78–83

"According to Caecelius of Caleacte": Athenaeus, 6, 104, 272f = FGrHist 183 F I.

"Posidonius, as we have seen, linked": in the account by Diodorus—whose source could have been none other than Posidonius—we read of "an abyss between slaves and masters," brought about by the mistreatment of the slaves, as the cause of "accumulated hatred: . . . the more the power of those who command is cruel and arbitrary, the more the behavior of those subjected to it, when driven to desperation, becomes ferocious": 34–35,2,26 and 33.

"To Lucretius": *De Rer. Nat.* 6,813–15 (with a correction of the manuscript tradition).

"to Strabo": 3,2,9.

"attention given by Thucydides": 7,27,5.

"reported by Livy": 3,15–18; 4,45,1–2; 22,33,1–2; 32,26,4–18: Capozza, *Movimenti servili nel mondo romano*, pp. 37ff.

"writes Diodorus": 34–35,2,25.

"Aristotle alludes to them": *Politics* 1,3,1253b.

"in Theopompus": FGrHist 115 F 122 = Athenaeus 6,88,265b–c; F 40 = Athenaeus 6,101, 271e, and F 176 = Athenaeus 6,101, 271d (without deleting "doulos," as Jacoby, and he alone, does in *Kommentar*, II, D, p. 382. For the thought of Posidonius, what can be deduced from Athenaeus is important: 6,84,263c–d = FGrHist 87 F 8 = Edelstein-Kidd F 60, compared with the episode in Diodorus, 34–35, 2, 20 and repeated in Athenaeus 12, 59,54b = FGrHist 87 F 7 = Edelstein-Kidd F 59 (good evidence of Diodorus's dependence on Posidonius).

"degenerate": the expression is used by L. Canfora, "La rivolta dei dannati della terra," in Diodorus, *La rivolta degli schiavi in Sicilia* (Palermo, 1983), p. 61, developing K. Reinhardt, *Poseidonios* (Munich, 1921), especially pp. 19ff., 31ff.

"declared aversion": Diodorus 34–35,25,1, again traceable to the philosopher.

Sec. 10, pp. 84–91

"shaken . . . by the disgrace": Plutarch, 9,8.

"We can estimate": P. A. Brunt, *Italian Manpower: 225 B.C.–A.D. 14* (Oxford, 1971; reprint with postscript 1987), pp. 449–450.

"correcting an oversight by Appian": E. Gabba, *Appiani Bellorum civilium* (Florence, 1958), pp. 321–322 (note).

"the figure mentioned by Orosius": 24,2.

"as Caesar": *De bello gall.* 1,40.

"as Cicero defined him": *Verr.,* 2,4,42.

"A fragment of Sallust": 3,106.

CHAPTER 3: THE LOSER

Sec. 1, pp. 92–96

"for Orosius it was four hundred": 24,3.

"Florus says the same": 2,8,11.

"from Ampelius": 45,3.

"the expression later used by Cicero": "faex urbis": *In Pis.* 9; *Ad Att.* 1,16,11; "perditissima atque infima faex populi" in *Ad Quint. Fr.* 2,4,5.

"in Eutropius and Orosius": 6,7,2 and 24,5. My comparison between Spartacus and Hannibal takes account of M. P. Fronda, *Between Rome and Carthage: Southern Italy during the Second Punic War* (Cambridge, U.K., 2010).

Sec. 2, pp. 96–103

"class consciousness": everything said in this section presupposes my analysis in A. Schiavone, *The End of the Past: Ancient Rome and the Modern West,* translated by M. J. Schneider (Cambridge, Mass., 2000; reprint 2002), especially chapters 8 and 10.

Sec. 3, pp. 104–108

"many of his [Mummius's] men were slain": Plutarch, 10,3.

"the City was hardly less afraid": Orosius, 24,5.

"Spartacus wanted to transform": see: Z. Rubinsohn, "Was the Bellum Spartacium a Servile Insurrection?" *Rivista di filologia* 99 (1971), pp. 290ff.; P. Piccinin, "Les Italiens dans le 'Bellum Spartacium,'" *Historia* 53, 2 (2004), pp. 173ff.

Sec. 4, pp. 108–113

"features not found again": once again I must refer, also in relation to what is said in the following pages, to Schiavone, *The End of the Past*, especially chapter 11, even if the perspective I am pursuing now is a little different to that reconstruction.

"exclusively to patrimonial issues": M. Finley, *The Ancient Economy*, 2nd ed. (London, 1985), pp. 35ff.; and M. Finley, *Ancient Slavery and Modern Ideology* (New York, 1980; expanded edition edited by B. D. Shaw [Princeton, N.J., 1998]), pp. 132ff. (though the idea was originally Weberian).

"a municipal Italic movement": E. Gabba, "Dallo stato-città allo stato municipale," in A. Schiavone (ed.), *Storia di Roma*, vol. 2, bk. 1 (Turin, 1990), pp. 697ff.; E. Gabba, "Rome and Italy: The Social War," in J. A. Crook, A. Lintott, and E. Rawson (eds.), *Cambridge Ancient History*, vol. 9, *The Last Age of the Roman Republic 146–43 B.C.* (London, 1994), pp. 104ff.; and E. Gabba, *Italia romana* (Como, 1994), pp. 14ff. See also E. Badian, "Roman Politics and Italians," *Dialoghi di archeologia* 4–5 (1971), pp. 373 ff.; and P. A. Brunt, *The Fall of the Roman Republic and Related Essays* (Oxford, 1988), pp. 93ff., 144ff., 240ff. A still-classic work is E. Lepore, *Il princeps ciceroniano e gli ideali politici della tarda repubblica* (Naples, 1954).

Sec. 5, pp. 113–117

"Few men desire freedom": 4,69,18.

"as Cicero writes": *De Dom.* 35, 94; *Pro Sest.*, 12, 27; *De Har. Resp.*, 21,45.

"the terrifying *res novae*": *Cat.* 28,4. Essential reading is A. La Penna, *Sallustio e la "rivoluzione" romana* (Milan, 1968), in particular, for our discussion, pp. 68ff. and 247ff.

"Tacitus also spoke": *Ann.* 15,46.

"prophetic and egalitarian vocation": the same egalitarian extremism opposed by Cicero. See, for example, *De rep.*, 1,53, about which La Penna, *Sallustio e la "rivoluzione" romana*, p. 135.

Sec. 6, pp. 118–122

"even in the slave revolts": K. R. Bradley, *Slavery and Rebellion in the Roman World, 140 B.C.–70 B.C.* (Bloomington, Ind., 1989), pp. 1ff.

"he proposed to encourage": Sallust, *Cat.* 24,2 (and see also 46,3 and 56,5): K. R. Bradley, "Slaves and the Conspiracy of Catiline," *Classical Philology* 73 (1978), pp. 329ff., and, once again, La Penna, *Sallustio e la "rivoluzione" romana*, pp. 295ff. On Gaius Gracchus, the Marians, and Cinna, who had tried, in extreme situations, to arm the slaves and stir up insurrections, but without great success, see Appian, 26,115; 57,262–263; 65,293–294; 69,316.

Sec. 7, pp. 122–131

"in the hands of Marcus Licinius Crassus": A. M. Ward, *Marcus Crassus and the Late Roman Republic* (Columbia, Mo., 1977), pp. 83ff.

"He seems to have taken advantage": the story is in Plutarch, *Crassus*, 2,5–6.

"all of those who, though advanced in years": Sallust, 4,21.

"about forty-five legions": P. A. Brunt, *Italian Manpower: 225 B.C.–A.D. 14* (Oxford, 1971; reprint with postscript 1987), p. 449.

"a different version": reported doubtfully by Appian, 118,550: E. Gabba, *Appiani Bellorum civilium* (Florence, 1958), p. 327 (note).

"for Orosius": 24,6.

"Florus": 2,8,13.

"Sallust": 4, 25–32.

"writes Cicero": *Verr.*, 2,5,4,8 (see also 4,9, which mentions the beginnings of a servile uprising).

"Publius Gavius": *Verr.*, 2,5,61,158–162,162.

"while in 72": *Verr.*, 2,5,36,95–37,98.

"Pyrganion": 6,3,5.

"But Sallust tells us": 4,32.

"betrayed him and sailed away": Plutarch, 10,7.

"Lucius Cecilius Metellus": Cassius Dio, 11,14,29.

"recount Sallust and Florus": 4,30 and 2,8,13.

"a fragment of Sallust": 4,29.

"Pliny calculated": *Nat. hist.* 3,73.

"Strabo even less": 6,1,5 (C. 257).

"Another brief fragment of Sallust": 4,31.

Sec. 8, pp. 131–137

"as Cicero claims": *Verr.*, 2,5,4,5–7.

"a better hypothesis": Gabba, *Appiani Bellorum civilium*, p. 328 (note). Also B. Strauss, *The Spartacus War* (New York, 2009), pp. 126ff.

"on 'a cold night'": Sallust, 4,35.

"a small military garrison": Sallust, 4,36.

"according to Frontinus": 1,5,20.

"(and, probably, Sallust)": 4,37.

"from fresh to salty": Sallust, 4,38 (besides Plutarch).

"Not a few publicly proclaimed": Plutarch, 11,8.

"Sallust writes": 4,39.

"trying to put some order into the accounts": Frontinus, 2,4,7 and 2,5,34; Plutarch, 11,4–5; Sallust, 4,40; Orosius, 24,6; Livy, *Periochae*, 97.

"would have come off badly": Plutarch, 11,5.

Sec. 9, pp. 137–145

"the mountains of Petelia": Plutarch, 11,6. (but cf. Strabo, 6,1,31 [C. 254]).

"if they did not conquer (Appian)": 119,553.

"Roman *fides* (Tacitus)": *Ann.*, 3,73.

"Caesar alone": in *De bello gallico* 1,40 (already mentioned). He in fact compares Spartacus's army to the Cimbri and Teutons defeated by Marius.

"as has sometimes been suggested": the reference is in Gabba, *Appiani Bellorum civilium,* pp. 330f–331. (note).

"One reliable hypothesis": Gabba, *Appiani Bellorum civilium,* p. 332 (note); Strauss, *The Spartacus War*, pp. 155ff.

"slew his horse": M. Capozza, "Spartaco e il sacrificio del cavallo (Plut. 'Crass.' 11,8–9)," *Critica storica* 2 (1963), pp. 251ff.; Strauss, *The Spartacus War*, p. 159.

"if he won the day": Plutarch, 11,9.

"'primo agmine'": Florus, 2,8,14.

"two versions": the first is from Appian, 119,557.

"The other": this is the one recorded by Plutarch: 11,10.

"writes Florus": 2,8,14.

"Sallust, more soberly but with equal respect, says": 4, 41.

"A Roman fresco": A. Maiuri, *Monumenti della pittura antica scoperta in Italia,* part 3, *Le pitture ellenistico-romane,* 2, *Le pitture delle case di "M. Fabius Amando," del "Sacerdos Amandus" e di "P. Cornelius Tega" (reg.1, ins.7)* (Rome, 1938); "J. Kolendo, Uno spartaco sconosciuto nella Pompei osca: Le pitture della casa di Amando," *Index* 9 (1980), pp. 33ff.; Strauss, *The Spartacus War,* pp. 182ff.

"crucified along the whole road": Appian, 120,559.

" 'extreme' and 'terrible' ": Cicero, *Verr.* 2,5,66,169: M. Hengel, *Crucifixion in the Ancient World and the Folly of the Message of the Cross* (Philadelphia, 1977), especially pp. 51ff.; see also Strauss, *The Spartacus War,* pp. 168ff.

"writes Suetonius": *Div. Aug.,* 3.

Sec. 10, pp. 145–149

"under the same roof": they are the words of the Senatus consultum Silanianum of A.D. 10, as can be gleaned from Ulpian, 50, *ad ed.,* in *Digesta* 29,5,1pr.

"no house": this is Ulpian again, in the text just cited.

"In A.D. 61": Tacitus, *Ann.,* 14,40–44.

"once again Augustus": with the *lex Fufia Caninia* of 2 B.C, which covered all the various cases with great precision (one hundred was the maximum): Gaius, *Inst.,* 1, 42–43.

"Tacitus reports": *Ann.,* 13,27: K. Hopkins, *Conquerors and Slaves: Sociological Studies in Roman History* (Cambridge, U.K., 1978), pp. 115ff.

SUGGESTED READING

What follows is simply a set of readings put together in relation to the interpretations presented in the book, and is not intended to be a bibliography on Spartacus, nor on Roman slavery.

It should be borne in mind that some of the background sketched out to give depth of field to the narrated events—especially in Chapter 3—presupposes two of my previous works: *La storia spezzata: Roma antica e occidente moderno* (Rome, 4th ed., 1999; reprint 2002), in English as *The End of the Past: Ancient Rome and the Modern West,* translated by M. J. Schneider (Cambridge, Mass., 2000; reprint 2002); and *Ius: L'invenzione del diritto in Occidente* (Turin, 2005), in English as *The Invention of Law in the West,* translated by J. Carden and A. Shugaar (Cambridge, Mass., 2012).

For an idea of the social and economic context in which our story takes place, see: A. Giardina and A. Schiavone (eds.), *Società romana e produzione schiavistica,* 3 vols. (Rome, 1981), especially vol. 1, *L'Italia: insediamenti e forme economiche,* and vol. 2, *Merci, mercati e scambi nel Mediterraneo romano.* For more on the political events, see A. Schiavone (ed.), *Storia di Roma,* 7 vols. (Turin, 1988–1993), vol. 2, bk. 1, *L'impero mediterraneo: La repubblica imperiale,* ed. G. Clemente, F. Coarelli, and E. Gabba (Turin, 1990); and *Cambridge Ancient History,* 2nd ed., revised and updated,

14 vols. (London, 1970–2001), vol. 9, *The Last Age of the Roman Republic 146–43 B.C.*, ed. J. Crook, A. Lintott, and E. Lawson (London, 1994), especially the essay by R. Seager, pp. 208ff. An excellent introduction to the themes dealt with in my book is M. Finley, *Ancient Slavery and Modern Ideology* (New York, 1980; expanded edition edited by B. D. Shaw, Princeton, N.J., 1998).

Then we can begin with T. Mommsen, *Roemische Geschichte*, 3 vols. (Leipzig, 1853–1856), in English as *History of Rome* (1866; digital reprint, Cambridge, U.K., 2009), translated by W. Dickson, pp. 78ff.; and with F. Münzer, "Spartacus," in *Realencyclopädie der Classischen Altertumswissenschaft*, vol. 3A, bk. 2 (1929), coll. 1527–1536; together with T. Rice Holmes, *The Roman Republic and the Founder of the Empire*, 3 vols. (Oxford, 1923), vol. 1, pp. 386ff.; and L. Pareti, *Storia di Roma e del mondo romano*, 6 vols. (Turin, 1953), vol. 3, *Dai prodromi della III guerra macedonica al "primo triumvirato" (170–59 av.Cr.)*, pp. 687ff.

Among more recent studies, I would mention K. Ziegler, "Die Herkunft des Spartacus," *Hermes* 83 (1955): 248ff.; J.-P. Brisson, *Spartacus* (Paris, 1959); G. Stampacchia, *La tradizione della guerra di Spartaco da Sallustio a Orosio* (Pisa, 1976), which provides very useful orientation in the mesh of sources; A. Guarino, *Spartaco* (Naples, 1979), the last Italian monograph written on the topic; M. Dogliani (ed.), *Spartaco: La ribellione degli schiavi* (Milan, 1997); B. D. Shaw, *Spartacus and the Slave Wars: A Brief History with Documents* (Boston, 2001), which is precise and informed; M. J. Trow, *Spartacus: The Myth and the Man* (Stroud, U.K., 2006), an easy and pleasant reading; M. H. Winkler, *Spartacus: Film and History* (Malden, Mass., 2007), a rich and interesting study; and B. Strauss, *The Spartacus War* (New York, 2009), a happy encounter for me when work on this book was already under way. See also P. Stothard, *Spartacus Road: A Journey through Ancient Italy* (New York, 2010).

Other useful works: B. Baldwin, "Two Aspects of the Spartacus Slave Revolt," *Classical Journal* 62 (1966–1967): 289ff.; M. I. Finley, *Ancient Sicily to the Arab Conquest* (London, 1968), chapter 11; B. A. Marshall, "Crassus and the Command against Spartacus," *Athenaeum* 51 (1973): 109ff.; J. Vogt, *Ancient Slavery and the Ideal of*

Man (Cambridge, Mass., 1975), pp. 39ff.; G. Stampacchia, "La rivolta di Spartaco come rivolta contadina," *Index* 9 (1980), pp. 99ff.; K. R. Bradley, *Slavery and Rebellion in the Roman World, 140 B.C.–70 B.C.* (Bloomington, Ind., 1989), especially pp. 83ff. Also worthy of attention are the proceedings of a conference on Spartacus held in Bulgaria in 1977: C. M. Danov and A. Fol (eds.), *Spartacus: Symposium rebus Spartaci gestis dedicatum 2050 A.* (Sofia, 1981), especially the contribution of F. W. Walbank, "Prelude to Spartacus: The Romans in Southern Thrace, 150–70 B.C.," pp. 14ff.

Finally, a number of studies are important for approaching the most important sources. For Appian, an essential work is E. Gabba, *Appiani Bellorum Civilium* (Florence, 1958), pp. 316ff. and 429ff.; and also, again by Gabba, *Appiano e la storia delle guerre civili* (Florence, 1956). For Plutarch: M. G. Bertinelli Angeli, *Plutarco. Le vite di Nicia e di Crasso* (Milan, 1993). For Sallust: B. Maurenbrecher, *C. Sallusti Crispi Historiarum Reliquiae,* Fasc. II: *Fragmenta* (Leipzig, 1893), pp. 146ff., 165ff.; A. La Penna, "Per la ricostruzione delle 'Historiae' di Sallustio," *Studi italiani di filologia classica,* new series, 35 (1963), pp. 5ff.; and, again by La Penna, *Sallustio e la "rivoluzione" romana* (Milan, 1968), pp. 247ff. For Florus: H. T. Wallinga, " 'Bellum Spartacium': Florus' Text and Spartacus's Objective," *Athenaeum* 80 (1992), pp. 25ff. For Livy's *Periochae:* L. Bessone, "La tradizione epitomaria liviana in età imperiale," *Aufstieg und Niedergang der römischen Welt,* vol. 30, part 2, bk. 2 (1982), pp. 1230ff. For Orosius: A. Lippold (ed.), *Le storie contro i pagani,* translated by G. Chiarini (Milan, 1976; reprint 1998), pp. 438–439.

INDEX

REVEALING ANTIQUITY

G. W. BOWERSOCK, GENERAL EDITOR